# THE RHYMNEY RAILWAY

## Volume 1

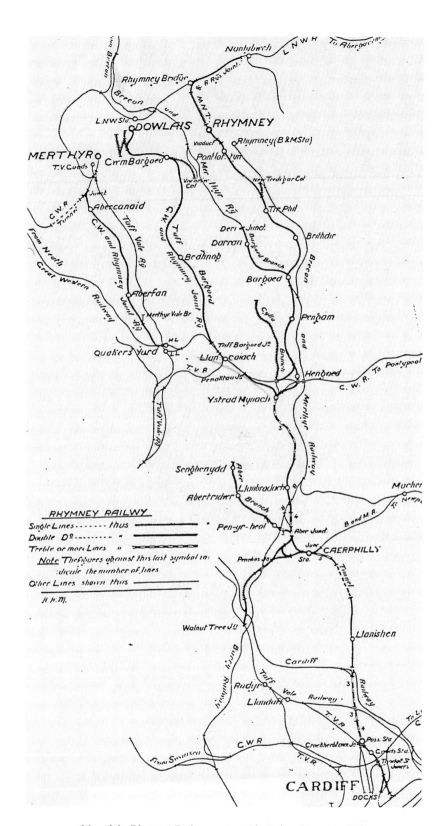

**Map of the Rhymney Railway system.** *The Railway Magazine, 1910*

# THE RHYMNEY RAILWAY

## Volume 1
## The main line from Cardiff

### John Hutton

·RAILWAY HERITAGE·
*from*
*The NOSTALGIA Collection*

First published in 2004

British Library Cataloguing in Publication Data

A catalogue record for this book is available from the British Library.

ISBN 1 85794 227 2

Silver Link Publishing Ltd
The Trundle
Ringstead Road
Great Addington
Kettering
Northants NN14 4BW

Tel/Fax: 01536 330588
email: sales@nostalgiacollection.com
Website: www.nostalgiacollection.com

Printed and bound in Great Britain

A Silver Link book
from
*The* NOSTALGIA *Collection*

*Page 1* The Rhymney Railway's seal as used on the side of its carriages. Although the chevrons have faded, much of the fine detail can still be seen.

The coat of arms has an interesting history; taken from the common seal of the company, according to the minutes taken at the first Board Meeting it was decided that it should be arranged as follows: Cardiff arms to the lower right of the seal, Newport arms to the lower left, surmounted by a vignette representing furnaces in the Egyptian style of architecture (this type of furnace was in use in the Rhymney Iron Works in 1828), a colliery on the right, and a ship to the left, to indicate the two terminals of the line. However, the engraver must have misunderstood the intention, for he placed on the left the seal that should have been on the right, and the colours of the Cardiff coat of arms are incorrect, as the chevrons should be gold. The placing of Newport on the shield is a mystery as the Rhymney Railway never went there. One wonders if is inclusion caused the first Marquess of Bute to turn in his grave!

The common seals of the company can be seen at the Great Western Railway Museum, Swindon, together with the seals of other railway companies that were taken over by the GWR both before and after the Grouping of 1922. I am indebted to Mr E. J. Starr, a former railwayman who once worked at the Caerphilly engine and carriage works.

*Below* Approaching from the south near Ystrad Mynach on the former Rhymney Railway main line on 6 June 1953 is ex-GWR '57xx' pannier tank No 3647 on a passenger service, looking hard-pressed as it climbs the gradient with its three-coach train. Heading south is another former GWR engine, a '56xx' Class 0-6-2T, hauling a mineral train comprising a number of 21-ton wagons and at least one 16-ton vehicle, all of steel construction. No 3647 was built at Swindon Works in 1939, and withdrawn in 1965. *The late N. L. Browne, courtesy of F. T. Hornby*

# CONTENTS

# FOREWORD

## by Alun Powell, retired railwayman

South Wales was a small railway kingdom in itself. Heavy industry in the valleys and the numerous coal-mines led to the construction of a most extraordinary complex of railway lines, many of which entailed extensive engineering work, such as earthworks, viaducts and tunnels.

One such railway was the Rhymney. With the completion of its first major step in 1858, from the town of Rhymney to the junction with the Taff Vale Railway at Walnut Tree Junction, Taffs Well, a new period in the history and development of the Rhymney valley was ushered in. The growth of the South Wales coalfield can only be fully understood when it is related to the story of its railways, and although the Rhymney only owned or shared just over 60 route miles, the volume of traffic carried in the heyday of its prosperity was out of all proportion to its size.

Unlike most of the railways in South Wales, the Rhymney did not follow the valleys down to the sea, thus securing a falling gradient for its loaded trains. Of the total length of Rhymney territory, shared or owned, only a few miles had gradients

less steep than 1 in 100. The Dowlais section of the Cwmbargoed branch rises continuously for 7 miles at 1 in 40, then falls towards Dowlais at 1 in 70, the station at Cwmbargoed being 1,250 feet above sea level, thus being one of the highest stations in Great Britain.

In this book you will find a living map of one of the country's most successful railways, created by a world mad for steam. The author has gathered together a fascinating pictorial record that will stir the memories of those who travelled and worked along the Rhymney Railway. The sudden plunge into the darkness of Caerphilly Tunnel never failed to thrill me, and visits to the Caerphilly works as a lad will always remain uppermost in my memories, while climbing up to Cwmbargoed from Nelson & Llancaiach station was as if one was going to the top of the world.

I hope that this book will bring lasting pleasure to all who scan its pages. John has often said to me that one picture is worth a thousand words, and with that I have to agree, as each photograph here has its story to tell.

A 'world mad for steam' needed access to the many collieries in the South Wales valleys, and one such was Llanbradach in the Rhymney Valley. On 27 April 1957 ex-

GWR 0-6-2T No 5687 heads a Cwmbargoed to Cardiff Docks freight, passing Llanbradach Colliery Sidings. The three- and two-plank 'coke raves' (side pieces) on the tops of the first, third and fifth wagons were fitted into place by the use of four T-shaped pieces of strapping that fitted inside both the coke raves and the body of the wagon and secured with nuts and bolts; they could thus be removed if the wagon reverted to ordinary coal or mineral use, albeit with some difficulty. This '56xx' Class engine was built in 1927 at Swindon Works, and was withdrawn in 1963. On the left can be seen a National Coal Board 0-6-0 saddle tank shunting on the network of colliery sidings. *B. J. Miller collection*

# HISTORY OF
# THE RHYMNEY RAILWAY

**P**rior to the opening of the Bute West Dock, Cardiff, in 1839, the Rhymney Ironworks, partly owned by the Marquess of Bute, had sent its products by tramroad to Newport. This tramroad was known as the Rumney Tramroad, but the Marquess made it known that once his docks were opened, the Newport situation would not continue. During the early 1840s, Bute negotiated with the Taff Vale Railway for the entire output of the Merthyr Ironworks to be sent to his docks at Cardiff, with a similar view for the output of his Rhymney works.

Robert Beaumont, mineral agent to the Marquess, tried to get Bute to build a railway up the Rhymney Valley, but His Lordship's purse was depleted owing to the expenditure involved in building the docks, so he would not consider it. Instead, he suggested that the Taff Vale Railway build a branch up the Rhymney Valley. The idea appealed, and the company drew up plans. However, Bute then objected on the grounds that a railway down the valley might be tapped by Newport – his aversion to Newport bordered on the paranoid – the result being that these plans never left the drawing-board. The Marquess died in 1848, so Newport remained the sole outlet from the Rhymney Valley.

Six years were to elapse before the idea of a railway from Rhymney to Cardiff arose once more, thanks to an active trustee of the infant Marquess of Bute, a Scotsman from Ayrshire, one John Boyle. He obtained an Act of Parliament for the building of a railway from Cardiff to the upper Rhymney Valley, and thus the Rhymney Railway was incorporated by an Act of Parliament on 24 July 1854. The preamble of the Act of Incorporation stated that 'a railway from Rhymney in the county of Glamorgan, to a point of junction with the Newport, Abergavenny and Hereford Railway, would be a great public advantage'. The original Rhymney Railway plan was to join up with the Taff Vale Railway at Nelson & Llancaiach, but this plan was rejected by Parliament, thus forcing the Rhymney Railway to re-think its plans, this time for an outlet to the south towards Cardiff. This amended plan was authorised on 2 July 1855, allowing the Rhymney to join the Taff Vale Railway at Walnut Tree Bridge, Taffs Well; this Act also included running powers over the Taff Vale Railway to the junction at Crockherbtown, in the town of Cardiff.

The Act also included two other elements. One was the making of a branch from Aber, the site of the first Caerphilly station, to coal workings at Wernddu. The other was the authorising of a branch from Crockherbtown to terminate at a new dock in course of construction, authorised by the trustees of the Marquess of Bute and called Bute East Dock; this line was some 1½ miles long from Crockherbtown, and 5 miles and 71 chains from Walnut Tree Bridge.

The making of this line from Aber to Walnut Tree Bridge, later renamed Walnut Tree Junction, was considerably held up by the excavation of a very deep cutting at Nantgarw, the alluvial nature of the soil creating considerable difficulties owing to the wet weather encountered. Excavation work was further delayed by the discovery of a substantial amount of quicksand in this area; the Act of Parliament and the contracts issued stated that this line was to be opened to traffic by 1856, but the delays held up the opening until February 1858, some considerable time later. Altogether the approach to Walnut Tree Bridge resulted in the excavation of one million cubic yards of material, and resulted in a failing gradient of 1 in 47.

The company built a stone single-road engine shed for the banking engines at Walnut Tree

Bridge in 1858, the allocation in May 1914 being Rhymney Railway engines Nos 35, 36 and 51. This engine shed closed in September of 1922, and was subsequently used by a nearby engineering firm; the shed survives at the time of writing, 82 years after closure.

In 1860 the Caerphilly branch was opened, much of the one million cubic yards of hard-won material from the Nantgarw cutting being used in the foundations of this branch, which extended eastward 1½ miles from Penrhos Junction to Caerphilly town.

The Rhymney's finances were always at a low ebb, but it still wanted a more direct line to the docks at Cardiff. After much wrangling with the Brecon & Merthyr Tydvil Junction Railway, which was encroaching upon Rhymney lines and which also wanted its own line to Cardiff, an opportunity was offered by the London & North Western Railway. Quickly taking full advantage of the LNWR's overtures, the Rhymney now had a strong and more financially sound partner and ally.

The Rhymney Railway opened its dock branch in September 1857, but the only traffic was freight via the Taff Vale Railway until the Rhymney opened its main line from Rhymney to Walnut Tree Bridge, which took place on 25 February 1858 for goods, and 31 March for passengers.

Originally the line from Rhymney to Walnut Tree Bridge was single throughout, and from Rhymney to Aber the engineering work was not too heavy, consisting of the construction of two viaducts, one at Pontlottyn, 360 feet long with ten arches, and a viaduct at Pont Aber Bargoed, known today as Bargoed, 333 feet long with seven arches, carrying the railway over the Rhymney River and a public road at a height of 66 feet.

In 1862 the LNWR leased the Merthyr, Tredegar & Abergavenny Railway, and gained parliamentary sanction on 25 July 1864 to build jointly with the Rhymney Railway a line from Rhymney to Rhymney Bridge, with the Rhymney company having running powers to Nant-y-bwch, a joint station on the MT&A line. In return this agreement gave the LNWR running powers from Walnut Tree Bridge to Crockherbtown. It was now abundantly clear that the LNWR was looking to Cardiff docks, for included in the 1864 Act was a new line of railway from Caerphilly to Cardiff;

without doubt it was the LNWR's much-needed financial help that would make this possible.

The work in connection with this new line into Cardiff, which would eventually become the present-day main line, involved the boring of Cefn On Tunnel, more than a mile in length, through the range of hills lying between Cardiff and Caerphilly, the excavation of a deep cutting, and the construction of a high embankment with a viaduct, situated 2 miles south of this tunnel; this embankment is known today as Heath High Level. The new main line was double track from its opening, on 1 April 1871, the distance overall from Rhymney to Cardiff being shortened by 1½ miles.

Regulations for the working of trains through the tunnel were very stringent. Goods or mineral trains could enter the north end of this tunnel at a speed no greater than 6mph, with sufficient wagon brakes pinned down so as to allow drivers to use a little steam while passing through the tunnel, but the speed of the train emerging from the south portal was not to exceed 4mph.

With the opening of this new line, Adam Street passenger station, at Crockherbtown, became goods only, with passenger services now using the Rhymney's new station, just to the north of the TVR's Queen Street facility. The new Rhymney station was called, at various times, Crockherbtown, Parade, and Cardiff (Rhymney). Meanwhile, Caerphilly's second Rhymney station was also opened, and at the same time the former running powers over the TVR line from Walnut Tree Bridge at Taffs Well were severed.

The Rhymney Railway now had a lot to celebrate, and had earned it with blood, sweat and tears. As for the LNWR, with the completion of Cefn On Tunnel and the line into Cardiff it opened a goods depot in the Bute Docks area, near Tyndall Street, and carried a large amount of traffic to and from the Midlands and North of England. This traffic had previously travelled over the Rhymney Railway's metals via the Hengoed Junction with the Newport, Abergavenny & Hereford Railway.

On 5 September 1871 the Rhymney Bridge branch was ceremonially opened; from Rhymney to Rhymney Bridge it was single line, but from there to Nant-y-bwch it was double track. Passenger services began on 2 October 1871.

The third notable line to open, on 27 September 1871, was the 1½-mile-long branch from Ystrad Mynach South Junction to Penalltau Junction, thus joining the Taff Vale Extension of the Newport, Abergavenny & Hereford Railway, which ran from Pontypool Road to Aberdare; prior to this the Rhymney had obtained running powers via Hengoed West Junction to Hirwaun, which resulted in the company gaining access to the mineral wealth of the Middle Duffryn Pits, in the Aberdare area, thus providing direct competition to the Taff Vale Railway, by carrying coal to Cardiff docks. This junction at Penalltau also allowed mineral and passenger traffic to and from the Taff Bargoed branch to reach Cardiff some five years later.

On 10 January 1876 the Taff Bargoed branch, belonging jointly to the Great Western and Rhymney railways, was opened, giving access to the large ironworks and collieries of the Dowlais Iron Company, later to be known as Messrs Guest, Keen & Nettlefold, situated at Dowlais, near Merthyr Tydfil. This branch, about 9 miles in length, commenced with a junction with the GWR at Nelson & Llancaiach, and rose continuously for a distance of 7 miles at a gradient of 1 in 40 to reach the station at Cwmbargoed, 2 miles from Dowlais and 1,250 feet above sea level. Up to 1910 the Rhymney Railway conveyed about 300,000 tons of iron-ore per year up this heavy gradient to the Dowlais Ironworks; only eight or ten 10-ton wagons were capable of being drawn by one engine, making the working of the branch very laborious and expensive. It opened for passenger services on 1 February 1876, the same year that the Rhymney Railway's mineral line from Cwmbargoed station to Fochriw Colliery opened.

In 1882 another joint line with the Great Western Railway was authorised. This was the Abercanaid branch in the Taff Valley, which finally opened to traffic on 1 April 1886. It crossed the River Taff by a stone viaduct at Quakers Yard and headed towards the village of Aberfan, where a short spur re-crossed the river to reach the Merthyr Vale Colliery of Messrs Nixon. The branch then continued to Abercanaid, just north of which another viaduct took the line to the Cyfarthfa collieries and ironworks of Crawshay Brothers at Merthyr Tydfil. The Rhymney Railway

joined the Hirwaun to Merthyr section of the GWR, the former Vale of Neath Railway, some 74 chains short of Merthyr High Street station – once again the Rhymney was close to Taff Vale Railway territory.

The Aber branch, for the development of the Aber Valley, located immediately north of Caerphilly, was authorised in 1890. Running from Aber Junction to the collieries at Senghenydd, this branch opened for the handling of mineral traffic and passenger services on 1 February 1894. However, some years previously, prior to the Act, a short length of track, of some 42 chains, leading from this junction to the Tregibbon Colliery, had been used for the handling of mineral traffic.

Three mineral-only lines were also opened. The Cylla branch, to develop the Cylla Valley north of Ystrad Mynach, was authorised by an Act of Parliament in 1895. This single-line branch ran from Ystrad Mynach North Junction, and was used in 1909 for the carriage of materials used in the sinking of a large colliery, later named Penalltau Colliery, for the Powell Duffryn Company; this colliery opened in 1906 and by 1910 was equipped to handle an output of a million tons of coal per year. A further 2 miles on was Penrhiwfelin Colliery; this section opened in 1909, and was closed a short time prior to the lifting of its rails in 1958. Situated about halfway along this branch was Cylla signal box, its Rhymney Railway nameplate reading 'Cylla Cabin'; this box closed in 1969, and the line to Penalltau Colliery was worked as a siding under the control of the signalman at Ystrad Mynach North signal box and the shunter. (In 1959 the goods yard situated opposite Cylla Cabin had been used by I. & R. Morkot to cut up a few former GWR locomotives, Nos 1418, 1436 and 5801.) Ultimately the branch was used by 'merry-go-round' coal trains to Aberthaw Power Station, but closure came in 1991, when Penalltau Colliery was the last one producing coal in the Rhymney Valley. British Rail placed the line out of use in November 1998.

Bargoed Pits branch, a short 32-chain mineral branch, was situated 2 miles south of Bargoed station, and gave mineral traffic from Bargoed Colliery access to the main line, under the control of the Bargoed Pits signal box at Bargoed South Junction. The Ystrad branch was a short connecting line between Ystrad North Junction and Hengoed West Junction to join the Taff Vale Extension line.

The New Tredegar Colliery branch was another short mineral branch, stretching some 60 chains to reach New Tredegar Colliery from a junction at Brithdir.

With the increasing volume of coal traffic, the main line between Caerphilly and Ystrad Mynach was doubled in 1873, and from Ystrad Mynach to Bargoed and Pontlottyn by 1892; however, the section between Pontlottyn and Rhymney remained single line.

The Darran and Deri branch consisted of 2½ miles of single track, and was opened in March 1864; it was doubled in 1909. Its end-on junction with the Brecon & Merthyr Railway at Deri opened a route to the mid-Wales section of the Cambrian Railways, and thus to the Midland Railway at Tal-y-llyn and Three Cocks Junction.

By the end of 1860 receipts from the handling of coal traffic exceeded all other types of traffic, and at the half year ending 31 December 1862 a dividend of 2 per cent was paid to the shareholders; subsequently, from 1863 to 1875 this dividend varied from nil to 3 per cent, then in 1876 it reached 4 per cent, climbing to 8 per cent in 1878, and 10½ per cent in 1880; by 1881 and 1882 these dividends reached a maximum of 11 per cent, dropping back to 10 per cent for three years afterwards.

In its heyday the main line and branches of the Rhymney Railway amounted to a total of 62 miles of track, with approximately 22 miles jointly owned with other railways. During 1908 the total tonnage carried over the Rhymney's lines amounted to more than 9,000,000 tons, the bulk of this traffic being coal for shipment from not only the Bute Docks of Cardiff, but also from the docks at Penarth and Barry.

Today the scene has changed dramatically, with many collieries and most lines closed. The main line, from Crockherbtown Junction at Cardiff, still passes through Cefn On Tunnel, en route to the now much depleted station at Rhymney. The line from Ystrad Mynach North Junction to the Taff Bargoed branch via Penalltau Junction can still be seen, but it only travels as far as Cwmbargoed and the open-cast mining site there; more often than not one will see more Ministry of Defence traffic using the line rather than coal trains. The West and East Bute Docks at Cardiff are no more, replaced by the Cardiff Bay development; the very few warehouses that survived were quickly converted into rather expensive flats. The original main line, which became the Walnut Tree branch, is now a pleasant cycle track and walk, part of the Taff Trail, while the Caerphilly branch has reverted to nature, except for the area near Penrhos Junction, which is now filled in and part of a new housing estate. The Abercanaid branch has been obliterated by the extension of the new A470 trunk road, which follows the River Taff, much as the Rhymney Railway did in better days.

The Aber branch has also mostly gone. Aber Junction is now a factory site and wagon park, and Abertridwr station and the nearby colliery site are now landscaped and built upon. The Cylla branch has had its tracks lifted, although the sleepers have been left, with buddleia – the favourite bush of butterflies and railways – growing in abundance. The Darran and Deri branch has also become a cycle track, part of the Northern Rhymney Valley countryside service; a short distance along the line, at Deri, can be seen the remains of a rather unusual Grade 3 listed bridge; however, its condition is deteriorating, and I feel that it is one thing to preserve a structure, but perhaps such orders should include protection as well.

# 1. THE MAIN LINE, CARDIFF TO RHYMNEY

The main line of the Rhymney Railway is still in use today, and in this chapter we will travel northwards up the Rhymney Valley, although it should be remembered that the Rhymney was one of the few railway companies to build its line initially at the top and work southwards. The line began to handle mineral and passenger traffic with the opening of Caerphilly Tunnel through the mountain at Cefn On on 1 April 1871.

## North from Cardiff

In 1924 *The Railway Magazine* reported, 'The layout of Cardiff Parade station is rather unusual. The older portion, opened in 1871, consists of the usual two platforms, but a new departure platform was added in 1908; this was placed on the arrival side, as there was no room for it elsewhere. Practically all northbound Rhymney trains use this platform, the older platform being reserved for the Cardiff Railway's railmotors, which have used this station since railmotor services started on the 1st of March 1911, under an agreement. For Cardiff, this station is a poor one and no one will regret it being closed.'

Cardiff Parade station was opened originally as Crockherbtown, being renamed Cardiff station in November 1888, and Cardiff Parade on 1 July 1924, on the same day that trains were diverted over a new junction into Queen Street Station, on the former Taff Vale Railway's line.

The Parade station closed to passenger services on 15 April 1928, and following demolition the GWR's S&EU club was built; Mr Llewellyn was the architect, and the contractors were Messrs I. E. Evans & Co. Well known to railwaymen as the

[8 Edw. 7.]     *Rhymney Railway Act, 1908.*     [Ch. xii.] *Nº 18*

#### CHAPTER xii.

An Act to authorise the Rhymney Railway Company to A.D. 1908. reconstruct their Cardiff Passenger Station to make a new railway to raise additional capital and for other purposes.     [18th June 1908.]

WHEREAS it is expedient that the Rhymney Railway Company (hereinafter called "the Company") be authorised to reconstruct and rearrange their passenger station at Cardiff and to make and maintain the railway hereinafter described :

And whereas plans and sections showing the line and levels of the railway authorised by this Act and also a book of reference containing the names of the owners and lessees or reputed owners and lessees and of the occupiers of the lands required or which may be taken for the purposes or under the powers of this Act were duly deposited with the clerk of the peace for the county of Glamorgan and are hereinafter respectively referred to as the deposited plans sections and book of reference :

And whereas it is expedient that the Company be authorised to raise further capital for the purposes of this Act and of their undertaking :

And whereas in or about the year 1891 the Company by agreement with the adjoining landowner and in accordance with the requirements of the Gelligaer Highway Board which was at that time the road authority for the district diverted the old public road crossing their railway on the level at or near Tyn-y-Graig Farm in the rural district of Gelligaer and Rhigos in the county of Glamorgan by constructing a bridge under their railway and forming metalling and completing and dedicating to the public a new road from a point near the said level crossing to and under the said bridge and thence over the adjoining lands to the old

[*Price* 1*s.* 3*d.*]     A     1ˌ

Act of Parliament, 18 June 1908, for the remodelling of the Rhymney Railway's Cardiff station. *Author's collection*

Parade railway staff club, it was opened by Sir William James Thomas, Bart, on 10 December 1932, and later became part of the British Rail Staff Club Association. It was demolished in 1989 to make way for the new university extension building.

*Below* Cardiff Parade station in June 1921, showing the exterior of the Rhymney Railway's main passenger station; this had replaced the original terminus in Adam Street, 14 chains southwards, which was thereafter used for goods traffic only. On the left of this photograph can be seen the arrival platform, and in the centre the departure platform. *The Transport Secretary*

*Below* Parade station c1910, looking north towards Crwys from the arrival platform. On the left can be seen the signals of the Taff Vale Railway, and part of the TVR's Crockherbtown Lower signal box. *The Transport Secretary*

*Above right* This Ordnance Survey map of 1922 shows the Rhymney station and Taff Vale station (later Queen Street) lower centre. The former Adam Street station can be seen above 'His Majesty's Prison'. Salisbury Road Depot, in the 'V' of Crockherbtown Junction, situated just north of Parade station, closed to goods traffic on 27 June 1966. Moy Road Sidings, at the top of the map, closed on 11 October 1965. Fairoak Road Cemetery Siding also closed on 27 June 1966. *Crown copyright*

*Right* An overall view of Crockherbtown Junction in October 1988. In the bottom right-hand corner can be seen the Parade railway club, with the university extension work creeping onwards. The DMU is travelling on the former joint Cardiff and Rhymney line and approaching Queen Street station, just out of view in the bottom left-hand corner. Going off to the left is the former Taff Vale Railway. It was at this junction that a connecting spur was put in by the GWR after the Grouping in 1922. *Author*

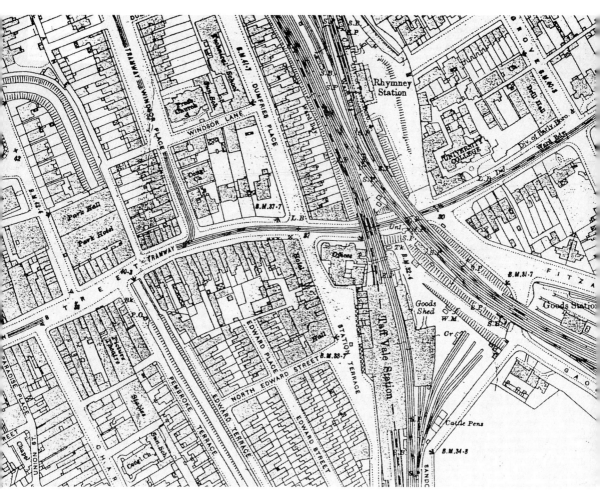

*Above*  A closer view of the area around the Rhymney's Parade and former Adam Street stations, and the Taff Vale station, in 1920. *Crown copyright*

*Below*  Crwys Coal Storage Sidings, c1905, looking southwards. The engine shed at Crwys opened in 1910, and closed in 1925. *From* The Railway Magazine, *1910*

*Below*  Circa 1963 0-6-2T No 5697 is seen at Crwys Sidings, with its driver, Viv Crabb, alongside. This '56xx' Class GWR engine was built in 1927, and withdrawn in 1963. *Viv Crabb*

*Right* No 5615 passes Heath Junction signal box on 30 May 1955 with a down passenger service to Cardiff. In the background is the former Cardiff Railway line leading to Coryton. This '56xx' engine was built in 1925, and withdrawn in 1963. *B. J. Miller collection*

*Right* Heath Junction signal box, reduced to 'HJ', seen c1978. This GWR-built box was opened in 1927, and closed in November 1984. *K. Ryan*

*Below* Rhymney engine No 15 hauls a Caerphilly to Cardiff Docks coal train at Heath South on 11 August 1913. Most of these seven-plank wagons are from the Powell Duffryn Collieries, but there are others whose initials are too faint to make out. This 'A Class'-design engine was built by Hudswell Clarke in 1911, works number 946, re-numbered 57 by the GWR. *LCGB, Ken Nunn Collection*

*Left* The Rhymney Railway line past Roath Park (centre), through Heath Junction (centre left) and Heath Halt, just to the north, in 1922. *Crown copyright*

*Above* Rhymney engine No 6, with the 6.56pm passenger train from Merthyr to Cardiff, passes the Heath area on 16 May 1919. This engine was built by the Robert Stephenson works in 1909, works number 3374, of 'P Class' design; it was re-numbered 83 by the GWR, and withdrawn from service in 1950. *LCGB, Ken Nunn Collection*

*Above right* Rhymney No 1, with a down passenger train in the Roath Park area, approaches Cardiff on 26 July 1922 after passing Heath High Level. *R. S. Carpenter*

*Right* Heath Halt opened in October 1915, and was re-named Heath Halt High Level station on 5 May 1969. Here it is seen on 18 March 1972, looking north towards Llanishen. Heath North Siding had closed to goods traffic on 30 July 1962. *J. C. Haydon*

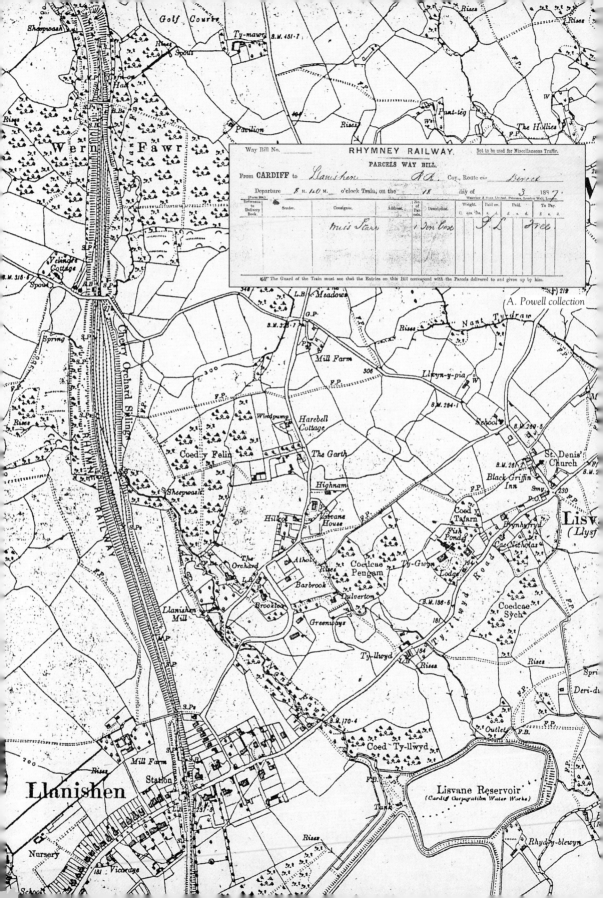

Way Bill No.

## RHYMNEY RAILWAY.

Not to be used for Miscellaneous Traffic.

### PARCELS WAY BILL.

From CARDIFF to *Llanishen* &c., Coy., Route *via* *Direct*

Departure 8 H. 40 M. o'clock Train, on the 18 day of 3 188 7

(Form 206.)

| Reference to Delivery Book. | Sender. | Consignee. | Address. | No. of Parcels. | Description. | Weight. C. qrs. lbs. | Paid on. £ s. d. | Paid. £ s. d. | To Pay. £ s. d. |
|---|---|---|---|---|---|---|---|---|---|
| | | Miss Stars | | 1 Tin Box | | | P.L. | Free | |

Waterlow & Sons Limited, Printers, London Wall, London.

☞ The Guard of the Train must see that the Entries on this Bill correspond with the Parcels delivered to and given up by him.

A. Powell collection

*Left* The line through Llanishen and Cherry Orchard Sidings, from a 1922 Ordnance Survey map. *Crown copyright*

*Right* Llanishen station, seen here c1900 looking south. The booking office was situated at street level, above the up-side platform, and was a rather massive stone-built structure. To reach the down platform travellers had to cross via the road bridge. Note the station name above the up platform waiting room, and the girls on the down platform wearing their smock frocks, a typical apparel for a Sunday or special day out. *Lens of Sutton collection*

*Right* The view from the road bridge, towards Cefn On, c1890. The goods yard is behind the up platform, while a rake of four-wheeled coaches stands in the station. *Lens of Sutton collection*

*Below* Passengers at Llanishen await the arrival of a Rhymney to Cardiff train in about 1900. A varied mixture of wagons waits in the goods yard bay siding. The up platform fence has been removed and the enamel advertising signs changed since the last view. The station closed to goods traffic on 27 June 1966, and the goods yard area is now a 'park and ride' facility, with the station handling passenger traffic only. *Lens of Sutton collection*

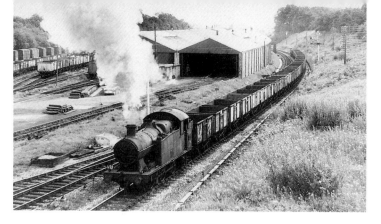

*Left* '56xx' 0-6-2T No 5635, with a rake of empty British Railways standard 16-ton mineral wagons, passes the sidings at Cherry Orchard on 19 August 1963, heading up the Rhymney Valley en route to Ogilvie Colliery. The large shed was used for the scrapping and breaking up of condemned wagons for scrap. By 1984 it was being used by Wales Gas for the storage of its equipment. This ex-GWR engine was built in 1925 and withdrawn in 1964. *B. J. Miller collection*

*Below* Where the locomotive was seen in the earlier picture has now become the site of Lisvane & Thornhill Station. On 28 October 1985 the finishing touches are being put to British Rail's new passenger station. In the background can be seen the former Cherry Orchard Sidings, part of which will be used for 'park and ride' facilities for the station. The station opened on 4 November 1985, with the Mayor and other dignitaries arriving on the newly designed 'Sprinter' DMU, No 150001, for the opening ceremony. Today a newly built housing complex stands where the sheds and sidings were. *Author*

*Below* Another view of Cherry Orchard Sidings, looking in the opposite direction c1963. Two DMU three-car sets coupled together are en route for Cardiff. In the background, beyond the second of the two signal boxes, is Cefn On Halt. Note the stripes on the front of the DMU, affectionately called 'cat's whiskers', and the backplate behind the signal arm, enabling the driver to see the signal arm more clearly against the structure of the overbridge. Cherry Orchard Sidings and Cefn On Sidings closed to goods traffic on 28 September 1964. Today they have been obliterated, not by man but by nature. *B. J. Miller collection*

*Right* Former Rhymney Railway 'R' Class No 40 hauls a Cwm Bargoed to Cardiff Docks freight, consisting of empty wooden wagons, slowly passing Cherry Orchard signal box and into the sidings on 12 August 1952. In the distance can be seen the shunter standing by the ground frame. This engine was previously numbered 44, built by Beyer Peacock in 1921, works number 6100, and rebuilt by the GWR on 21 May 1930; it was withdrawn in 1952. *B. J. Miller collection*

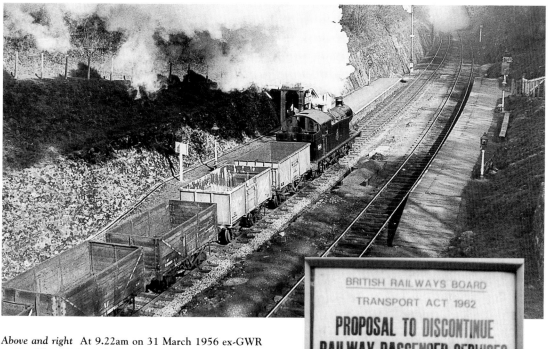

*Above and right* At 9.22am on 31 March 1956 ex-GWR engine No 6619 is about to pass through the rather picturesque Cefn On Halt before entering Caerphilly Tunnel with a rake of Crwys Sidings to Llanbradach Colliery empties; the smoke from a down train has obscured the tunnel entrance. The first two wagons are of the British Railways standard 16-ton steel type, with two 13-ton open wooden seven-plank wagons behind them; these are loose-coupled wagons, which, when full, could create havoc for an inexperienced engine driver or guard on a descending gradient. The halt's ticket office was on the up platform; those travelling to Cardiff would have to cross the road bridge after purchasing their ticket, as there was no footbridge here. This '56xx' Class engine was built at Swindon Works in 1928, and withdrawn in 1963. Cefn On Halt (spelled 'Cefn Onn' by BR from the 1960s) was opened in October 1915. Eventually, after an objection was submitted by one person, it closed on Saturday 27 September 1986, after which trains called at the new Lisvane & Thornhill station, as proposed by the poster photographed in February 1986 outside Cardiff Queen Street station. *B. J. Miller collection/author*

# Caerphilly

The new Caerphilly station opened on 1 April 1871, more suitable for the increased passenger traffic that was expected now that the more direct route to Cardiff was open. The *Cardiff Times* on that date carried the announcement of the new line and station at Caerphilly, replacing the Walnut Tree Junction route, and the first trains to use the station were decorated with flags. It was also noted that the new fares were not cheap – even a Saturday market day return was tenpence. On 8 August 1871 the *Cardiff Times* stated that the first Station Master would be Mr Wright, formerly of Walnut Tree Bridge, and on 17 March 1877 the paper informed its readers that the old station was to be demolished, as it was unsuitable for the increased amount of passenger traffic that had built up with the new line.

In 1973 British Rail began a three-year reconstruction scheme, costing nearly three-quarters of a million pounds, to improve conditions at and provide a new image for the stations and facilities covering the Taff Vale, Rhondda and Rhymney Valleys. Unfortunately this meant that the character of many of the old stations was destroyed; the old booking offices and waiting rooms, many still in their original styles, especially those of the Rhymney Railway, were demolished and replaced with modern BR shelters, which provide no more shelter from inclement weather than a bus shelter. Similarly, disused sidings and goods yards were ripped up, levelled and re-surfaced to provide 'park and ride' facilities for six stations on the former Rhymney lines: Rhymney, Hengoed, Pontlottyn, Llanishen, Ystrad Mynach and Tirphil. At Caerphilly a bus terminal and an old people's home now occupy the former goods yard site.

This view of Caerphilly Station is from about 1910, looking towards Rhymney. The bracket signal at the end of the up platform reads (left to right) up main to loop, up main line, and up main line to down siding, while the signal past the road bridge is for the down main. On the right are the goods yard sidings, and just in view behind the advertising posters can be seen a cattle truck of Rhymney Railway design. *Lens of Sutton collection*

Caerphilly station was re-designed in 1913, becoming the largest station on the Rhymney Railway system, with five platform faces serving four through roads, and a bay line on the down side. On 26 April 1960 a DMU heads southward towards East Junction, which is just past the goods yard. Seen in the background is East Junction signal box, which opened in 1913 with 162 levers, and was the largest on the Rhymney lines; it closed on 19 July 1964. *B. J. Miller collection*

A 1922 Ordnance Survey map showing lines around Caerphilly. On the right the line emerges from Cefn On Tunnel and passes the Rhymney Railway Locomotive Works before arriving at the station. The branch south towards Walnut Tree Junction heads west, and curving to the north is the new main line to Walnut Tree Branch Junction and on to Ystrad Mynach. *Crown copyright*

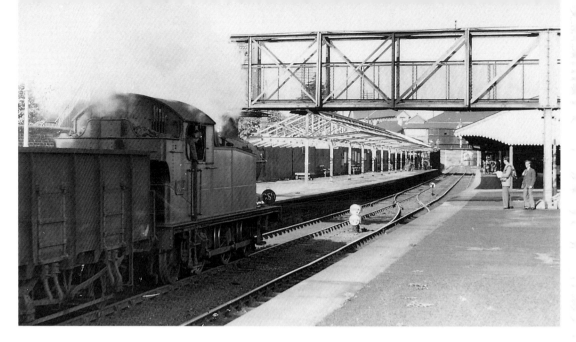

*Above* On 14 August 1954 0-6-2T No 6635 passes westward through Caerphilly Station with coal empties heading up the valley; built at Swindon Works in 1928, this locomotive was withdrawn in 1964. The wagon behind it is a British Railways standard 21-ton mineral wagon of the double-door type, of all-steel construction. *The late N. L. Browne, courtesy of F. T. Hornby*

*Below* In 1973 Caerphilly station went through another major alteration programme. A new ticket hall replaced the booking office located on the Cardiff Road railway bridge, being placed adjacent to the bus station; one of the existing down platform buildings became the new waiting room, and on the up side the old buildings were demolished and replaced by a new waiting shelter. Other parts of the station were repainted and improved lighting was installed. In this 12

March 1985 photograph, the bus terminus covers the former goods yard area, and the erstwhile booking office is now a shopping complex. *Author*

*Right* The network of lines immediately west of Caerphilly in 1922. The original Rhymney Railway route passes from the top to the bottom left, with the new station at the eastern apex of the Walnut Tree Branch Junction/Caerphilly Branch Junction triangle. Immediately south of Caerphilly Branch Junction is Penrhos Junction, and immediately north of Walnut Tree Branch Junction is Aber Junction, where the Senghenydd branch curves away in the top left-hand corner. On the left is the Barry Railway's route heading south towards Walnut Tree. Behind the Station Inn was the location of the first Caerphilly station. *Crown copyright*

*Above* Aber Halt in about 1960, looking towards Caerphilly. This halt opened in April 1908 as Beddau Halt (spelled Beda in *Bradshaw* up to June 1908), was re-named by the GWR as Aber Junction Halt on 17 September 1926, and re-named again by British Railways to Aber Halt on 6 May 1968, gaining its present name of just Aber on 5 May 1969. It is still in use for passenger services today, but the old corrugated iron shelters are gone, replaced by the modern open greenhouse-style of shelter, with a typically modern British Rail booking office on the down platform. *Lens of Sutton collection*

*Left* An early photograph of Aber Junction and sidings in about 1905. *From* The Railway Magazine, *1910*

*Left* Aber Junction signal box in September 1984, seen in its re-built GWR design. Looking north, a DMU is en route for Rhymney. This signal box closed in May 1987, and although the main line is still in situ, today everything else has gone, the sidings are built upon and the DMUs have been replaced. *Author*

*Right* Beyond Caerphilly the Rhymney Railway entered an area dense with collieries and ironworks, as the following maps show. The first is Campion's Map of the Collieries, Ironworks and Stations in South Wales, circa 1884. Caerphilly is in the centre of the lower half. *Author's collection*

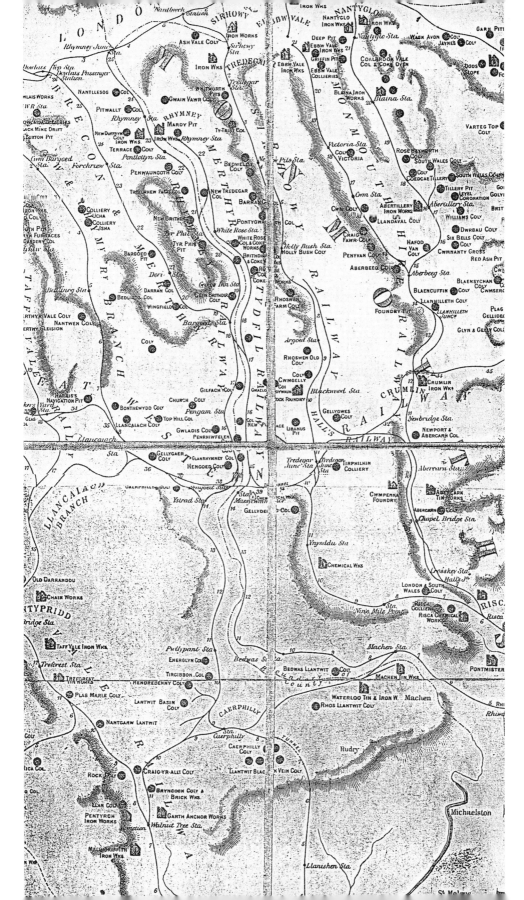

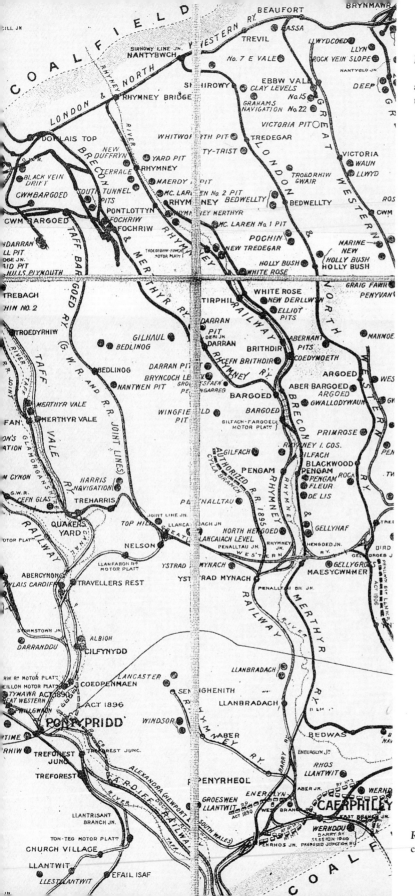

*Left* A Taff Vale Railway district map of 1910, showing the Rhymney Railway and associated lines from Caerphilly northwards. *Author's collection*

*Right* Gordon's map of the South Wales coalfield in 1921. *Author's collection*

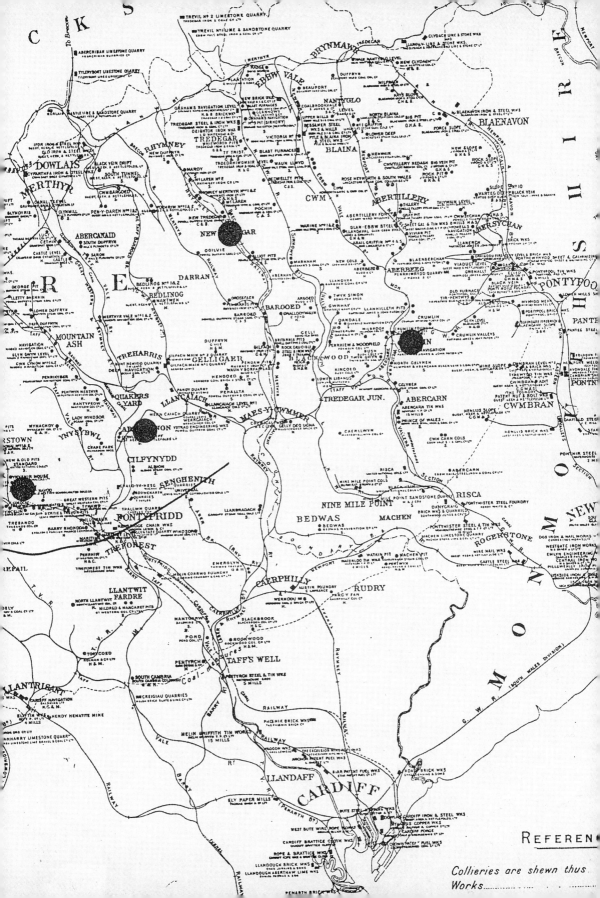

P474

F.S.

S.P.

271

1484

1494

1483

Pwll-y-pant
House

1475

268

S. P.

Pwll-y-pant
Station

1496

S. P.

1476

322

1452

M.P.
B.M.358.2
S.P.

Cardiff Doo

1451

Level

Chimney

gine House

Shaft

Well

Energlyn
Colliery

1477

1478

1481

**Left** Just north of Aber Junction was Energlyn Colliery, shown at the bottom of this 1873 Ordnance Survey map. Just to the north is Pwll-y-pant station. *Crown copyright*

**Below** The '56xx' Class engines were used extensively in the valleys of South Wales, and were good workhorses, reliable and strong – on the Rhymney lines they needed to be. No 5600, the first of the class, is seen here with a Cardiff to Bargoed Pits freight, passing Energlyn Sidings and heading up-valley on 2 May 1959. No 5600 was built at Swindon Works in 1924, being withdrawn in 1962. *B. J. Miller collection*

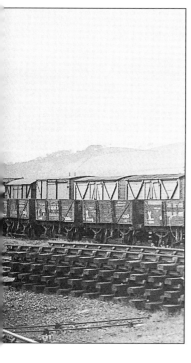

**Right** This 1936 Ordnance Survey map shows the site of Energlyn Colliery at the bottom, and the Rhymney line heading northwards through Llanbradach. On the right is the Brecon & Merthyr Railway, and leaving it to cross over the Rhymney and run parallel with it southwards is the Barry Railway. A station at Pwll-y-pant (centre) opened in 1871, closing to goods and passenger services on 1 March 1893 when it was replaced by the new station at Llanbradach, 58 chains to the north. *Crown copyright*

*Above* This is Llanbradach station, looking south towards Pwll-y-pant Quarries c1900. On the left, behind the down platform, can be seen the goods shed, long since demolished and with a housing estate now occupying the site. Llanbradach was typical of the staggered or split platform layout that the Rhymney adopted whenever possible, especially up the valley, perhaps to save money but more likely to suit the contours of this terrain. The platforms were usually connected by a footbridge. Opened on 1 March 1893 for goods and passenger services, Llanbradach closed to goods on 5 April 1965, but is still in use for passenger services. *Lens of Sutton collection*

*Below* Another view of Llanbradach station in about 1950, this time facing north towards Ystrad Mynach. The photograph has been taken from the end of the down platform, with the up platform on the left; the latter's waiting room is in blue pennant stone, probably from the nearby Pwll-y-pant quarry, edged with the yellow engineering brick that was used extensively by all railways throughout the country. By the look of the discarded paving slabs and the sack or hand trolley, it looks as though the down platform has been resurfaced with tarmac, and a newly painted platform edge applied. *Author's collection*

*Above* Llanbradach Colliery is seen c1910, with a rake of workmen's coaches in the siding on the right. This colliery was sunk in 1885, and production ceased on 29 December 1961. The buildings were demolished on 27 February 1965. *Mid Glamorgan Libraries*

*Below* Llanbradach Colliery Sidings were photographed on 27 April 1957 (see also page 6). NCB engine *Lundie*, built by Andrew Barclay & Sons at the company's Caledonian Works, Kilmarnock, is shunting a rake of wagons carrying Scandinavian pit-props on the colliery's internal lines. *B. J. Miller collection*

(393) 10/19.

No. 6303 RHYMNEY RAILWAY.

Excess Fare Receipt issued at YSTRAD MYNACH

Train 8.40    Date 31.7 1920

Ticket held by Passenger } from _____ to _____ No. _____

Excessed from _____

| Cause of Excess. | No. of Passengers (in words). | | Excess Fare. | | |
|---|---|---|---|---|---|
| | Single. | Return. | £ | s. | d. |
| Class without tickets | two | | | 1 | 0 |
| „ travelled on ... | | | | | |
| Second to First ......... | | | | | |
| Third to First ............ | | | | | |
| Third to Second .......... | | | | | |
| Class child over age | | | | | |
| | | | | | |

Collector.

This through Ticket is issued subject to the conditions and regulations referred to in the Time Tables, Books, Bills and Notices of the respective Companies and Proprietors on whose Railways, Coaches, or Steamboats it is available and the holder by accepting it agrees that the respective Companies and Proprietors are not to be liable for any loss, damage, injury, delay, or detention caused or arising off their respective Railways, Coaches or Steamboats. The contract and liability of each Company and Proprietor are limited to their own Railways, Coaches and Steamboats.

# Ystrad Mynach to Bargoed

*Above* Ystrad Mynach station opened on 31 March 1858 as Ystrad, being re-named Ystrad Mynach on 1 December 1891. The staggered platform arrangement can be seen quite clearly in this photograph of the station in about 1920, looking north towards Hengoed. On the extreme left is the 'Dowlais' platform, serving the line to Penalltau Junction, for passengers en route to Dowlais Cae Harris or Merthyr. *Lens of Sutton collection*

*Left* An Excess Fare Ticket issued at Ystrad Mynach on 31 July 1920. *J. C. Haydon*

*Below* The second view, looking in the opposite direction in about 1960, serves as a good reminder of just how busy the sidings were at Ystrad Mynach, with fully loaded coal wagons waiting to be taken to the docks at Cardiff or Barry. The station closed to goods traffic on 20 September 1965, but is still in use for passenger services. *Lens of Sutton collection*

*Above* On 7 September 1957 a former Rhymney Railway 'R' Class engine, with GWR number 36, is seen with a Cardiff to Bargoed Pits freight, passing the down platform at Ystrad Mynach. South Junction and the line to Penalltau Junction can be seen on the extreme right, and on the left are the extensive Ystrad Mynach Sidings. No 36 was originally Rhymney Railway No 40, built by Hudswell Clarke, works number 1432, in 1921. *B. J. Miller collection*

*Below* A similar view in March 1985 shows, on the left, the remains of the sidings behind the down platform. The full extent of the changes at this location can be realised when compared with the previous photograph. *Author*

*Top* Hengoed station opened on 31 March 1858, originally as Hengoed, later re-named as Hengoed & Maesycwmmer on 1 June 1905, then Hengoed Low Level on 1 July 1924, finally becoming Hengoed again on 6 May 1968. Its goods facilities closed as long ago as 1 November 1925. This photograph shows Hengoed Low Level station on 10 July 1958; the High Level station serving the Taff Vale Extension line, which crossed the Rhymney by the bridge seen in the background, towers above. The platform canopy is of the typical Rhymney Railway style. On the right, on the other side of the fencing, are the sidings linking the Taff Vale Extension and Rhymney lines; it was at this point that the Rhymney Railway joined the Taff Vale Extension line of the Newport, Abergavenny & Hereford Railway, as laid down in the 1854 and 1857 Acts of Parliament. *H. C. Casserley, courtesy of R. M. Casserley*

*Middle* Pengam station opened on 31 March 1858. Originally known as Pengam, it was re-named as Pengam & Fleur de Lis on 1 February 1909, reverted to Pengam under the GWR on 1 July 1924, changed to Pengam Glam on 29 March 1926, and lastly became Pengam once again under British Rail on 6 May 1968. Goods facilities were withdrawn on 28 September 1964, and Pengam signal box closed on 5 April 1965, but the station is still open for passenger services. Photographed in the 1950s looking south towards Hengoed, at the far end of the down platform was the entrance to the goods yard, part of which today is a police station compound. *Lens of Sutton collection*

*Bottom* A second view of Pengam station at about the same time, looking towards Gilfach Fargoed. Gas lamps are still in use, ignited or extinguished by the station staff on duty at the time. *Lens of Sutton collection*

*Right* A 1938 Ordnance Survey map showing the route of the Rhymney Railway between Hengoed (bottom) and Pengam. *Crown copyright*

# Bargoed

*Left* Bargoed and its pits in 1945. The opening of the Rhymney Railway in 1858 enabled the coal cut out from the upper coal series of the Rhymney Valley to be carried to Cardiff, originally via the Nantgarw cutting at Penrhos. In 1871, after the opening of the Cefn On Tunnel, the number of collieries in the Caerphilly basin increased to eight, and by 1876 this had become twelve. In 1886 the Energlyn Coal Company produced 35,702 tons of coal and the Rhos Llantwit Coal Company 46,156 tons. The collieries at Fochriw, Cwmbargoed, Bedlinog and Nantwen were owned by the Dowlais Iron Company, while the collieries at Abercanaid and Treod-y-rhiw (which included the Castle Pit and Gethin Pit) were owned by the Cyfarthfa Iron Works. In 1935 these collieries became subsidiaries of the Welsh Associated Collieries, finally merging with Powell Duffryn Limited to become part of the National Coal Board in 1948. *Crown copyright*

*Top* Gilfach Fargoed Halt, just below the centre of the map opposite, was photographed in the 1950s, looking south towards Pengam, during platform re-surfacing work. The halt opened in April 1908 as a railmotor halt, and still in use today as a request stop. *Lens of Sutton collection*

*Middle* Another view, taken in December 1985, providing an overall view of Gilfach Fargoed Halt, with DMU set C305 approaching with a down-valley service. *Author*

*Bottom* On 9 May 1959 another GWR '56xx' Class engine, No 5635, passes Bargoed South Junction with an up-valley freight at Bargoed. This engine was built in 1925, at Swindon Works, and withdrawn from service in 1964. Bargoed South Junction signal box opened in 1890 and closed on 28 January 1968; as well as Rhymney line traffic it controlled movements to and from Machen via the connecting line to the former Brecon & Merthyr route in the valley. *B. J. Miller collection*

*Left* Bargoed Pits signal box controlled access to the colliery. Opened in 1903, it closed in October 1975, and is seen here in January 1982. The Bargoed Pits shaft was sunk in November 1901, production beginning the following year. The colliery closed in December 1983. *P. Korrison*

*Below left* Bargoed Coke Ovens. The wagons are Stephenson Clarke 20-ton steel vehicles, and their livery is black overall with plain white lettering. *Stephenson Clarke Ltd*

*Below* A bird's eye view of the extensive sidings network of the Bargoed Coke Ovens. These two photographs appeared in **Model Railway News** in June 1965. *Stephenson Clarke Ltd*

*Below* On 7 September 1957 an ex-GWR '56xx' Class hauls a down-valley mineral train at Bargoed Pits. *B. J. Miller collection*

*Above* Bargoed station c1890, looking south. The station opened on 31 March 1858 as Bargoed; re-named Bargoed & Aberbargoed on 1 June 1905, it reverted to Bargoed on 1 July 1924. Goods facilities were withdrawn on 22 March 1965, but the station is still open for passenger services. The booking office was on the down platform; note the gas lamps and platform trolley, and South Junction signal box, which can be seen in the distance through the road bridge arch. *Lens of Sutton* collection

*Below* At Bargoed in about 1906 a Rhymney Railway engine arrives with an up-valley passenger service. The arched stone-built road bridge, seen in the previous photograph, has been replaced by a more substantial girder bridge with additional spans to support the new booking office. The station nameboard reads 'Change for Brecon & Merthyr and Cambrian Railways'; the platform for these connections was situated behind the board, where the B&M trains arrived via Bargoed South Junction. *Lens of Sutton collection*

*Left* An early postcard view of Bargoed station looking north from the road bridge before rebuilding. 'Bargoed Junction' on the station nameboard is puzzling, as there is no record of the station under that name. The closest reference I have found is in the 1864 Act of Parliament, which gives an indication of the possible date of this postcard: 'The authorised junction between the Brecon and Merthyr line, near Pont Aber Bargoed, to be abandoned, a substituted junction to be made south of Bargoed Station, according to a plan to be arranged between the two companies. The Rhymney Company to give the Brecon Company running powers between the abandoned and substituted points of junction, including use of the Bargoed Station.' *Lens of Sutton collection*

*Left* Looking north from the down platform c1910, in the distance can be seen the North Junction signal box. The saw-tooth valance has only been half painted – perhaps the painter was having lunch when this photograph was taken! Numerous enamel advertising signs decorate the stone-based water tank building, as well as the down-side booking office. In the distance the driver of an unidentified Rhymney engine can be seen awaiting instructions from the signalman. *Lens of Sutton collection*

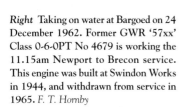

*Right* Taking on water at Bargoed on 24 December 1962. Former GWR '57xx' Class 0-6-0PT No 4679 is working the 11.15am Newport to Brecon service. This engine was built at Swindon Works in 1944, and withdrawn from service in 1965. *F. T. Hornby*

*Right* Bargoed station goods shed, photographed in January 1970. Today these premises are occupied by a vehicle dismantling firm. *P. Korrison*

*Right* Bargoed North Junction signal box, seen in January 1982, had closed on 9 November 1970. *P. Korrison*

*Below* During the singling of the line from Bargoed to Pontlottyn in 1970, the North and South Junction signal boxes at Bargoed were closed. To replace them, the signal box that was originally at Cymmer Afan was transferred, rebuilt and opened for use on 9 November 1970. The new box is seen here in June 1985. *Author*

*Top* Brithdir station opened in 1871. Originally known as George Inn, it was re-named on 1 October 1891, and is still in use for passenger traffic, although it lost it goods services in April 1957. Seen here looking north c1910, on the left is the entrance to the goods yard. The signals on the right control the down main line (upper arm) and the down goods loop; the signals are of the centre-pivoted 'somersault' type, much favoured by the Rhymney Railway as well as other lines. Beyond them can be seen the down-side waiting room. *Lens of Sutton collection*

*Middle* Another photograph of Brithdir station, c1930. An abundance of enamel advertising signs cover the up-side waiting room wall: Nestlé's milk and Bovril were as popular then as they are 70 years later. In the distance is what looks like an approaching down-valley train, but on closer examination it is not on the main line but behind the wooden lineside fence. Brithdir North and South Junction signal boxes both closed in February 1932, replaced in that month by a GWR 'B'-type signal box, which itself closed on 4 March 1969. *Lens of Sutton collection*

*Bottom* Tirphil station opened on 31 March 1858 as Tirphil & Tredegar, being re-named Tirphil on 1 July 1924. It closed to goods traffic on 4 January 1965, and its signal box closed in November 1970, but the station is still open for passenger services. The original Rhymney Railway buildings were demolished in the 1970s when the line was singled; the down platform and waiting room are seen here on 30 June 1963. A milepost marker can be seen attached to the waiting room wall, beside which are two station trolleys; these were heavy to pull even without a load, especially if these cast-iron wheels were stiff due to lack of grease. *J. J. Davis*

*Right* Tirphil, from an Ordnance Survey map of 1938. *Crown copyright*

*Right inset* Tirphil goods shed, photographed on 22 April 1979. *M. Lloyd*

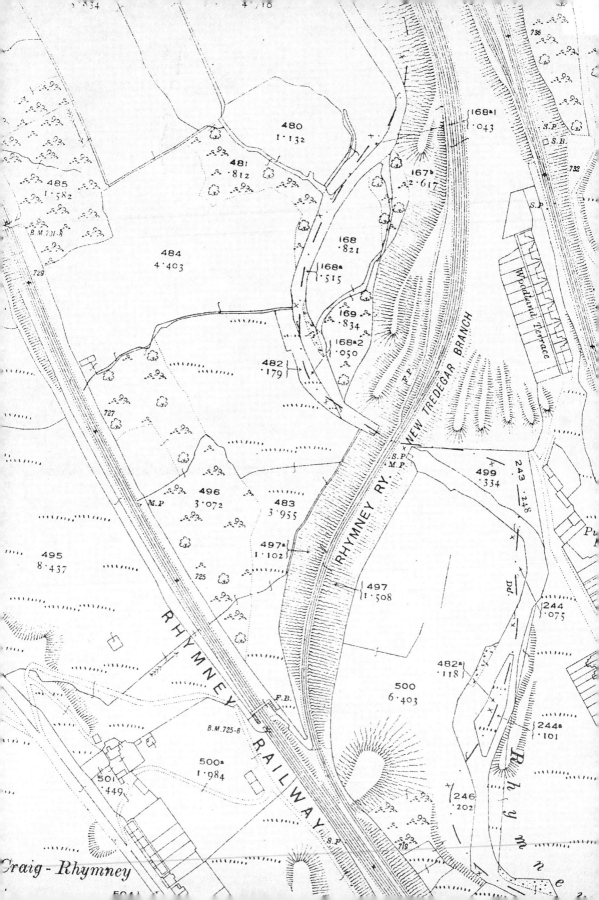

480
1·132

481
·812

485
1·582

484
4·403

B.M.731·8

729

482
·179

168
·821

168ª
·515

169
·834

168·2
·050

167ᵇ
2·617

168·1
·043

S.P.

S.B.

Woodland Terrace

S.P.

732

736

727

P.P.

NEW TREDEGAR BRANCH

S.P.
M.P.

499
·334

243
·248

Dd.

244
·075

M.P.

496
3·072

483
3·955

497ª
1·102

497
1·508

RHYMNEY RY.

482ª
·118

244ª
·101

495
8·437

725

500
6·403

246
·202

Rhymney

RHYMNEY RAILWAY

F.B.

B.M.725·6

500ª
1·984

501
·449

S.P.

Craig - Rhymney

500

*Left* A closer view of the junction north of Tirphil of the Rhymney Railway's New Tredegar branch – a location also served by the Brecon & Merthyr Railway – from an Ordnance Survey map of 1919. The Act of Parliament of 25 July 1864 stated that the receipts arising from traffic carried between the New Tredegar works and Cardiff shall, as between New Tredegar and Caerphilly, be divided in equal proportions between the two companies, after a deduction of 30 per cent for working expenses. The mileage proportion between Caerphilly and Cardiff was to belong exclusively to the Rhymney Railway, the Brecon company being allowed working expenses on the portion carried by them. Also mentioned was that until the first day of July 1865, the Brecon company was not to use the running powers mentioned for New Tredegar traffic.

Running powers can be a bit confusing; however, the Act explained the agreement clearly: 'The running powers granted by one company to the other shall include the use of sidings, watering places, and supply of water when required, and the use of stations shall include all proper office, warehouse, siding, and other accommodation, including standing room for engines, with full and proper access necessary for conducting the traffic, and power to appoint booking and invoice clerks.' *Crown copyright*

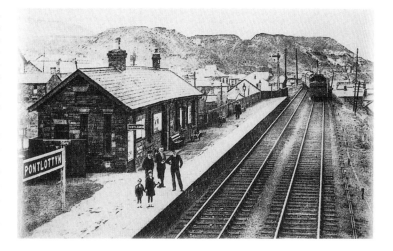

*Top* Pontlottyn station opened in 1860 and the up-side waiting room and station staff are seen here c1904, as a down passenger train approaches the station, having just crossed Pontlottyn viaduct. Pontlottyn Colliery, known as the Rhymney & Merthyr Colliery, opened in 1891, closing in the 1920s. To serve it, Pontlottyn Colliery Platform was opened between Tirphil and Pontlottyn on 1 January 1916, but was closed by September 1928. Reed's paper mill and other factory units now cover the site of the former colliery. *H. F. Jones*

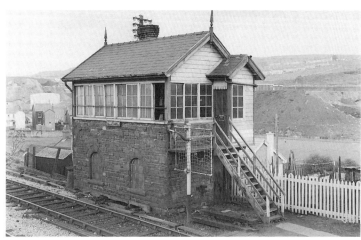

*Middle* The staggered platforms at Pontlottyn, looking south c1910. The station lost its goods facilities on 27 November 1967, but is still in use for passenger services. The warped roof of the up-side waiting room lasted until demolition in the 1970s. *Lens of Sutton collection*

*Bottom* Pontlottyn North signal box on 31 May 1969. It opened in 1890 and closed on 9 November 1970; Pontlottyn South signal box had closed on 24 May 1945. *J. J. Davis*

Track-lifting of the former down line between Bargoed and Pontlottyn took place during the weekend of 7-10 November 1970. Seen here is a Class 37 locomotive with the engineer's train. The second view shows track removal in progress shortly after the completion of the singling operation. *Both B. Morris*

## Rhymney

On Saturday 27 February 1858 the *Cardiff & Merthyr Guardian* printed this short piece on the Rhymney Railway:

### OPENING OF
### THE RHYMNEY RAILWAY TO CARDIFF

It is with unfeigned pleasure that we congratulate our townsmen on the opening of the Rhymney Railway, the entire length, 23 miles long, thus throwing open to our docks new and important coalfields, which may be said to be inexhaustible. This gratifying event took place on Thursday last in a very modest and unpretending manner.

It being the wish of the directors, we understand, that no public demonstration should be made on this occasion, in fact the opening of the line was kept so profound a secret that scarcely more than a dozen persons in Cardiff were aware that Thursday had been fixed for it. The opening was made by two trains, one of iron and one of coal, passing down the entire length of the line, from Rhymney to the terminus at the East Bute Dock, the former consisted of twenty-four trucks laden with one hundred and fifty tons of Rhymney Company iron, and the latter of forty mineral wagons of coal,

containing two hundred and forty tons, from Mr Thomas Joseph's colliery at Craig Rhymney.

The trains were under the immediate direction of Mr Thomas Clements, the locomotive superintendent of the line, who drove the first engine up the line to Caerphilly on Wednesday.

On the tender of the first engine on Thursday we observed Mr W. H. Page, the general superintendent, Mr Smith, civil engineer, and Mr Jackson, the contractor.

The trains were gaily decked with a profusion of flags and evergreens, and their appearance in the town created quite a commotion in those streets adjoining the railway.

The line has now been formerly opened for coal, iron, iron ore and general merchandise traffic, and we understand passenger trains will commence running in about three weeks or a month hence.

The works on the Rhondda branch to Mr John Edwards's collieries will now be pushed forward with the greatest energy, and when complete will form a very important feeder; other branch lines to collieries will also be constructed, and thus the rich mineral district through which the line traverses will be developed, and ere another summer's sun has passed over Cardiff, our East dock will be competing with our West dock in the bustle and excitement of prosperous trade, and will require the second extension, now in the coarse of construction, to be made for the increased accommodation of the magnificent ships visiting our port, which is now becoming one of world-wide fame. When our East Bute Dock is thus completed, Cardiff will then be in the proud position of having the finest sheet of enclosed water in the United Kingdom, covering an area of fifty acres including basin and locks.

Then on Saturday 6 March 1858 the same newspaper reported on the half-yearly meeting held at Westminster, attended by the directors of the Rhymney Railway Company to discuss the various problems that had been faced and overcome with the building of their new railway and the future mineral traffic that it would carry:

## THE RHYMNEY RAILWAY
## FROM RHYMNEY TO CARDIFF

The half-yearly meeting of this company was held on Saturday at the office in Great George Street, Westminster, Mr J. Boyle in the chair. The report stated that the Rhymney Iron Company were prepared to send their traffic over the main line when opened to Bute Docks. Arrangements were in progress at the collieries upon the line for bringing on traffic, and a very extensive steam coal colliery in the upper part of the valley had been opened, from which a large daily quantity would probably be sent to Cardiff. The railway would afford to the public the shortest route, without break of gauge, from the Port of Cardiff to Hereford, Chester, Liverpool, Leeds and other important towns and districts in England.

The northern part of the line from Rhymney to the Hengoed Junction with the Newport, Abergavenny & Hereford Railway, a distance of upwards of nine miles, had been opened for minerals and other goods traffic for some weeks, and minerals had been sent by that route to Newport and Staffordshire.

The Bute Dock Branch had been ready for some time, but the traffic from the Taff Vale Railway destined for that branch had not hitherto been carried over it, in consequence of a charge for services at the junction proposed to be made by the Taff Vale Railway Company, to which the directors had been advised not to assent.

The capital account showed that £2485 45s had been received and £2475 15s spent, leaving a balance of £130.

The chairman, in moving the adoption of the report, stated that the main line was opened to Cardiff on Thursday last, and would have been opened earlier but for the occurrence of the slip on the large cutting at Nantgarw. Their line would receive some of the surplus traffic of the Taff Vale Railway, but since the opening some difference had arisen with respect to the toll, which the directors had resolved to pay, but under protest, and if persisted in then it must be charged to the freighters.

The Rhymney Iron Company had sent over their line, the first day, 150 tons of iron, the Welsh iron ore required to be mixed with foreign iron ore, and they would have a large traffic from that source. He then referred to the various sources from which they would derive traffic, and hoped they would soon have authority from the government inspector to carry passenger traffic.

In reply to a question, it was stated that the line had cost much more than the original estimate, partly in consequence of the erroneous calculation of the former engineer, and partly because of the very high prices they had to pay for land. The whole expense would be about £400,000, and cost per mile about £16,000.

Resolutions were passed adopting the report, re-electing Mr W. Austen, M. J. Boyle and Mr Cave, the retiring directors, and Mr Watkins, the retiring auditor. A vote of thanks to the chairman closed the proceedings.

Rhymney Station opened on the 31st of March 1858, using the premises of the old school, the pupils having to go to another school situated at Twyncarno Village, this station eventually closed to the handling of goods traffic on the 15th of June 1964, still in use for passenger services.

196

*Reservoir*

*Rhymney Station*

*Level*

C.R.

B.M. 875.1

198

.871

968

*Shaft*

Shaft

*Engine House*

*Old Dyffryn Pit*
(Coal)

Air Shaft

C.R.

S.P.

*Level*

Spring

Shaft
199

Coke
Furnaces

Saw Mill

B.M. 872.0

B.M. 957.9

*Coke Furnaces*

Blast Furnaces

200

Limekiln

*Old Quarry*

**Rhymney Iron Works**

Blast Furnace

*Reservoir*

Old Quarry

General View of Rhymney No. 1.

*Left* Rhymney station (top) and Iron Works seen in an Ordnance Survey map of 1873. *Crown copyright*

*Above* This c1937 view of Rhymney station, looking north, is exceptional, showing the south end of the station. The GWR signal box on the left has not long been opened. A mixture of coaching stock can be seen: at the side of the goods shed is a rake of four clerestory coaches, the one at the right-hand end being an all-3rd vehicle. In the centre of the view is either a 16-ton or 24-ton GWR-built brake-van, in the middle distance can be seen GWR loco coal wagons, and in the far background are a mixture of private owner coal wagons, their initials quite clearly seen, from left to right

'GLM', 'SC' and 'WAC'. Today none of the buildings are left, and only a scattering of lines survive, some of which are carriage sidings, while the rest come to a dead stop just past Rhymney station's platforms. *Lens of Sutton collection*

*Below* Another overall view, this time looking south, c1958. Left to right can be seen the stone building comprising the down-side waiting room and booking hall, coaches in the goods yard sidings, then the up-side platforms and waiting room. Two coaches can be seen at the Rhymney Bridge platform, and behind them is the original Rhymney Railway engine shed, which closed in March 1965. To the right is the water tower, located in front of the carriage shed. *The late Mr Glyn Davies*

*Left* A ground-level view of Rhymney station, c1900, looking south. Nearest the camera is the platform face for trains northward to Rhymney Bridge, with its waiting room. Under the arch of the footbridge can be seen tarpaulin-covered wagons in the goods yard sidings. The signal in front of the camera is of LNWR design. *Locomotive & General Railway Photographs*

*Left* This view shows the rear, or north, end of the engine and carriage sheds, photographed on 25 July 1922, with Rhymney Railway engine No 37 'on shed'; built in 1921 by Hudswell Clarke, works number 1456, it was re-numbered by the GWR as 80. Just behind this engine is the water tower, and on the right, behind the coal wagons, is a Rhymney Railway 14-ton brake-van. *R. S. Carpenter*

*Below* Looking north towards Rhymney Bridge on 15 September 1963, the DMU is forming the 3.15pm service from Rhymney to Cardiff Queen Street. *J. C. Haydon*

*Top* Rhymney engine shed, signal box and sidings, looking south on 20 January 1968. The engine shed closed in March 1965, and when photographed it had already suffered a fire that gutted almost all of it. *M. Lloyd*

*Middle* A closer view of Rhymney signal box, on 30 July 1963. Opened by the GWR on 22 November 1936, it replaced the original Rhymney Railway signal boxes, Rhymney Viaduct, Rhymney No 1 and Rhymney No 2, which all closed on that day. This box was closed by British Rail on 28 May 1972. *J. J. Davis*

*Bottom* Behind the signal box was Rhymney engine shed, seen here on 6 April 1953 with a mixed trio of engines: on the left is ex-GWR '51xx' Class 2-6-2T No 4143, built at Swindon Works in 1946 and withdrawn in 1964, then the former Rhymney Railway 'P' Class loco No 6, built in 1909 by Robert Stephenson, works number 3374, and numbered 82 by the GWR, and on the right a former Taff Vale Railway engine, No 11, built by Hawthorne Leslie in 1914, works number 3060, and numbered 393 by the GWR. *F. T. Hornby*

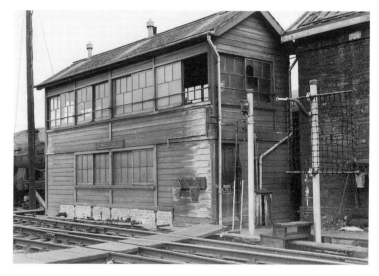

*Above* At Rhymney's Diesel Sub Depot on 16 July 1967 are three English Electric Type 3s, later Class 37s, D6879 leading. On the left is a DMU, with its 'whiskers' (see page 20) now replaced by a yellow warning panel. *F. T. Hornby*

*Below* Rhymney goods shed as it looked in April 1985. *Author*

# 2. RAILWAYMEN

*Above* Mr Ernest Albert Prosser, General Manager of the Rhymney Railway. *From* The Railway Magazine, *1910*

*Above right* Mr John Kendal, Locomotive Superintendent of the Rhymney Railway until his death in a railway accident in 1869 (see Volume 2, page 32). *From* The Railway Magazine, *1910*

*Right* Mr Henry (Harry) Roberts often took his shunting horse home with him, and became a familiar sight riding it through Caerphilly and down Van Road to the sheds each morning. Mr Roberts was one of the last people to be invested for bravery by Queen Victoria, in 1900, just before her death. He can be seen in old newsreels of the funeral procession at the side of the funeral carriage, in full military uniform, accompanying the late Queen to her last resting place at Frogmore, Windsor. The exact nature of his bravery award is not known, but he was the youngest person to have received it. *A. Carreg*

**Left** In the shunting yard of Caerphilly Works in about 1935 are, from right to left, Harry (Tai) Roberts, Trevor Roberts, Douglas (Dai) Stone, John (Jack) Roberts, and a foreman called Jack – two brothers, a brother-in-law, and an uncle. Harry and Trevor Roberts spent many years in the goods yard and sheds at Caerphilly, working and maintaining 'the Old Puffin' Bills', as they affectionately called them. They were from an old Caerphilly family, and their father, Henry (Harry) Roberts, seen on the previous page, came down from Cheltenham in the 1920s to join them at Caerphilly. They are standing by former Rhymney Railway engine No 112, built by Hudswell Clarke in 1908, works number 847, of 'S' Class design; re-numbered by the GWR as 609, it later became No 94. *A. Carreg*

**Left** On 27 June 1963, an unknown railwayman is flanked by, on the left, fireman Ray Cook and engine-driver Viv Crabb. In the background is engine No 5648, at Crwys Sidings. *Viv Crabb*

**Right** Mr Walters and the goods yard staff beside the shunters' office at Aber Junction, c1968. *G. Morgan*

*Above*  The interior of Pontlottyn signal box and Mr Islwyn Davies, the signalman on duty. This photograph was taken on 8 November 1970, the last working day before closure. *B. Morris*

*Right*  Part of the Rhymney Railway Company's Agreement with their employees, 1 January 1910. *Courtesy of T. D. Chapman*

*Below*  Committee members of the Cardiff Parade Railway Staff Club, photographed in January 1989. Left to right they are Jack Brown, Charlie Lock, Mervyn Searle, Harry Sanctuary, Cliff Whiting, Paula Harris, Bob Payne (standing), Walter Sinclair, Glyn Harding, Eddie Charles, Eric Jones, Bill Davies (standing), Councillor George Davies, and Glyn Hill. *Author, with thanks for the names to Mr M. O'Connel, club chairman, Great Western Railway Staff Association, Cardiff*

AMALGAMATED SOCIETY OF RAILWAY SERVANTS
OF
ENGLAND, IRELAND, SCOTLAND, & WALES.

Head Offices:—72, ACTON STREET, GRAYS INN ROAD, LONDON, W.C.
TELEGRAPHIC ADDRESS: "BEWARE." LONDON.

In reference to your                                    Branch

Address   Caerphilly
          y Hantgarw Caerphilly

                              Aug 27 1900

A letter from the Caerphilly Branch of the Amalgamated Society of Railway Servants (part of the NUR from 1913), offering support to their Taff Vale Railway colleagues on strike of August 1900.

'Dear Mr Bell

Referring to TVR strike and the possibility of some of their traffic coming in contact with RR signalmen.

I wish to draw your attention to the Pontypridd, Caerphilly & Newport railway, should an attempt be made to run traffic from Pontypridd to Newport by either TVR, GWR, Alexandra Dock or B&M companies.

This matter was discussed at my Branch last night and instructions were given the signalmen that are members of the ASRS not to take block for such a train, but we have two signalmen at Penrhos Jct that are not members of our Society, this is the first cabin that they would come in touch with.

I should like to have your advice to these men.

Wishing you and all the men every possible success.

Yours faithfully

Dave Thomas, Branch Secty

PS Rhymney railway platelayers had a meeting at Hengoed last Saturday, which I understand by D. Williams that you are aware of. They passed a resolution that if a satisfactory reply is not to hand by next Saturday they consider the advisability of signing their notices. I may say that we had a verbal reply [?] that 1/- advance all round would be granted.

I have not asked sanctions from you for a movement in as much that since the failure [?] of the recent South Wales movement a lot of the men left the service and many of the others left the Society, but there seems a move again amongst the new Blood, we had 11 new members at Saturday's meeting, I trust that should they come out on strike that something will be done for those that are members of the Society.

Dave Thomas

This strike involved the famous Taff Vale Judgement, whereby the TVR was granted an injunction against the ASRS establishing that a trade union could be sued and legally restrained from picketing and offering violence to those who remained at work. National Union of Railwaymen

# 3. TUNNELS, BRIDGES AND VIADUCTS

## Caerphilly Tunnel

As early as 1854 there were letters in the *Cardiff & Merthyr Guardian* concerning the possibility of the tunnel, one on 11 February '…advocating. the construction of such a tunnel, in that Robert Clive MP of St Fagans, whose family owned land in Caerphilly, chaired a meeting at the Cardiff Arms Hotel, to consider a railway which would commence with a junction in the Rhymney valley.' It was intended to join the Taff Vale Extension from Newport (the Abergavenny and Hereford portion, then still under construction). Among those present were Mr William Goodrich of Energlyn, Mr Evan Evans, Mr Thomas Reynolds, and Mr Thomas Anthony, all Caerphilly men of substance.

However, in 1861 the proposed Rhymney Railway Bill was thrown out by the House of Lords, reported the *Cardiff Times* on 26 April, and it was not until several attempts later that the Bill was passed in 1864 (*Cardiff Times*, 27 May). The same paper, on 5 August, reported that the Rhymney Railway company agreed to construct a new line to Cardiff with branches to Aber and Gledyr, on the strength of the prospect of increased business, and a new branch of the Cardiff Bank of Wales was opened in Caerphilly, the manager being Mr Joseph Evans.

At a Board of Directors meeting on 9 May 1865, a tender of £46,953 was accepted from Messrs Griffiths and Thomas. Further Directors' minutes record progress on the work:

**13 June 1865:** Mr Griffiths now asks for extra cash as he now estimates the contract will cost not less than £62,500. Rhymney Board of Directors accept this increase after hearing the opinion of Mr Lundie, engineer for the company.

**24 April 1866:** Mr Lundie, authorised to see Mr Easton Gibb (of Aberdeen) and negotiate £5000 from the contract figure

**8 May 1866:** letter from Mr Gibb states that he disapproves of this, but accepts the new proposals that shares still held will be redeemed if unsold after three years.

**12 June 1866:** Mr Thomas Barrows appointed Inspector of Works in the tunnel, with Mr Lundie, engineer under contract.

**1 August 1866:** Mr Gibb agrees to complete contract in 2½ years instead of the previously agreed 3 years (Tunnel Contract No 3).

**12 November 1867:** Tenders accepted for sections 1 and 2, of 1½ miles of the Cardiff to Caerphilly Railway, and awarded to Messrs Griffiths and Thomas (of Newport); Contract No 1 awarded to John Logan and James Hemingway for £84,395; Contract No 5 awarded to Logan and Hemingway for £23,178; Contract No 4 awarded to Mr J. J. Walker, of Cardiff, for £16,263.

**14 January 1868:** Award of £6,000 increase on Mr Gibb's contract price.

**14 April 1868:** Tender for two girder bridges at a cost of £360 for the Cardiff to Caerphilly extension line awarded to Messrs Parfitt and Jenkins of Cardiff.

**9 February 1869:** Further consideration to an extension of time on the Logan and Hemingway contract for the tunnel centre.

**23 February 1869:** Further meeting – two contracts of Messrs Logan and Hemingway to be rearranged.

**9 March 1869:** Mr Lundie directed to explain the decision to rearranging of contracts, and why he suggested that there is a termination of contracts on 30 April 1870.

**24 August 1869:** Logan and Hemingway asked to make a conditional contract for extension of tunnel, if needed.

*Above* The south portal of Caerphilly Tunnel seen from Cefn On Halt, c1956. *B. J. Miller collection*

*Below* The north or Wernddu end of Caerphilly Tunnel, in June 1984. With the opening of this new line on 1 April 1871 the transformation of the short spur to the Wernddu Brickworks was complete, as it became part of the new main line. A short distance from the Wernddu Brickworks is Wernddu Cottages, built by the Rhymney Railway from stone excavated from the tunnel. *Author*

**13 September 1870:** Extension of tunnel northwards, by some 40 feet, more or less, and to employ the contractors of the tunnel to make this extension.

**14 March 1871:** Minutes state that on 23 September 1870 the notice of the proposed opening date had already been given to the Board of Transport, and the second notice was now also to be given.

**11 April 1871:** Minutes state that the Cardiff to Caerphilly Railway has been opened for traffic since 1 April 1871.

**11 June 1871:** Logan and Hemingway make extra claim for expenses, incurred due to the tunnel consisting of stone and not the expected clay and sand; claim declined by the Board, who in return are prepared to forego their own penalties for failure to execute the contract in the time stated. On 10 February 1874 agreement was reached with Messrs Logan and Hemingway and the seal of the Rhymney Railway was attached.

Meanwhile the *Cardiff Times*, on 13 July 1866, reported that because of the dispute between the contractors and the Rhymney Railway, the work was suspended, but on 10 August it was stated that the firm of Logan and Hemingway had taken over and work had resumed during the week-ending 24 August. However, according to the paper it was not until February 1867 that contractors started to erect wooden huts for the accommodation of workmen engaged to build Cefn On Tunnel, and on 4 July 1868 the *Cardiff Times* reported that a start had been made on the building of Caerphilly station (the present site) and also on the Railway Hotel.

The Cefn On construction camp was the temporary abode of many navvies, whose toughness was a byword, causing consternation wherever they went. The earning capacity of these itinerants was dependent on the amount of earth they could shift; two men, usually working to a truck to contain their spoil, often shifted 30 tons of earth per day between them. The ground to be excavated was undercut with pick and shovel, the navvies jumping for their lives as the earth fell. Tunnelling was considered the most hazardous work undertaken by the navvy; falls of rock and the descent by bucket down the access shafts caused many accidents. According to the *Cardiff*

*Times* (10 August 1866), there are five of these shafts at Cefn On, varying from 43 to 117 yards in depth.

The construction of the tunnel was difficult and occupied nearly five years; many problems were encountered and the work was fraught with danger, a heavy flow of water having to be dealt with, as well as a large opening in the mountain that abounded with fissures on the Cefn On side. In addition, limestone, which connected with other fissures extending towards the surface of the hill, became mixed with mud and running sand, which rushed out upon the workmen, exposing them to considerable danger and partially filling the completed portion of the tunnel; the sheer volume checked the pumps and covering them so as to render them inaccessible.

Large springs of water were also encountered, which needed constant pumping; at one period the northern half of the tunnel quickly filled with water, which rose to a considerable height in the working shafts, bringing operations at that end of the tunnel to a standstill for nearly three months. The water was eventually capped and, by means of pipes laid along the railway from the centre of the tunnel, provided an abundant supply of good water, which was conducted towards Cardiff – about 60 million gallons per year for the use of the Rhymney Railway engines stationed at Cardiff, as well as for other purposes.

The arduous work and the risks undertaken made accidents inevitable. For example, on Monday 14 January 1867 Henry Cole, a ganger working on No 4 shaft, died, crushed by machinery in the engine house. On 9 August 1870 the *Cardiff Times* reported that Cefn On had long been a favourite picnic site. As many as 2,000 members and friends of the Oddfellows Friendly Society (Caerphilly area) visited in 1861, and the tunnel works provided an added attraction. Many people went to see the powerful steam engines that raised the spoil up the shafts, and some pencilled their names and passages of scripture on the contractors' staging.

The first train to carry passengers through the tunnel ran on Saturday 3 December 1870. This special train left Cardiff for Caerphilly, and, according to the *Cardiff & Merthyr Guardian*, carried Mr Lundie, the traffic manager, other officials, and a large party of ladies. On 1 April

1871 the *Cardiff Times* carried the announcement of the opening of the new line and the station at Caerphilly, to replace the Walnut Tree Junction route. The first train to be officially used for passenger services was decorated with flags, and a new chapter in the history of the Rhymney Railway had begun.

Caerphilly Tunnel was re-centred during Sunday 2 March 1947, raising the clearance to a height of 18ft 6in, 4 inches higher than previously. This work on the inside of the tunnel had to be done as a matter of some urgency, as falls had occurred, and the affected portions had to be made secure without delay, especially as some of the brickwork of the centres was sagging, ready to drop. Mr Jones noted in his engineer's report that the 4-inch clearance had been obtained with difficulty.

Today the maintenance gangs carry out regular work checking and relining the tunnel. At the Cefn On end the water that seeps through the tunnel roof has now been diverted via drainage pipes to soak into the ground, thus keeping the brickwork and track fairly dry.

## ALARMING INCIDENT ON THE RHYMNEY RAILWAY

### COMING TO A STANDSTILL IN A TUNNEL.

On Friday evening a somewhat alarming incident occurred on the Rhymney Railway, but fortunately without any serious consequences. The last up passenger train leaving Crockherbtown Station, Cardiff, at 7.15 for Rhymney, after entering the Caerphilly tunnel, at a distance of about 800 yards from the south entrance, suddenly came to a standstill, which naturally caused great excitement among the passengers, who feared that something of a serious nature had occurred. However, through the promptitude and presence of mind of Mr. David Jones, the guard, the panic was allayed. He immediately left the van, carrying with him a lamp, and informed the passengers that the cause of the stoppage was a mishap to the air-brake. The train within a few minutes was re-started.

*Above* Report from the *Pontypridd Chronicle* of 27 February 1885. *Pontypridd Library*

*Left* An engraving of the opening ceremony of the Bute East Dock Extension, on 19 January 1858. In the background can be seen the viaduct that carried the Rhymney Railway's iron and coal wagons over to the hoists and sidings located on each side of the dock. A close examination shows an engine crossing the viaduct and heading north back towards the Rhymney Valley. *The Illustrated London News Picture Library*

## Bargoed Viaduct

The dangers of building railways in areas of widespread coal-mining are exemplified by the case of Bargoed Viaduct. On 30 December 1921 Mr L. Snell, of the Rhymney Railway Permanent Way Department in Cardiff, wrote a letter to Mr W. G. Griffiths of Cardiff, regarding Bargoed Viaduct:

Dear Sir
When inspecting the road at this place, this morning, I found signs of some movement taking place which effects the Bargoed Viaduct; so far it is not very pronounced but it appears to me that the centres of the two northernmost arches have a tendency to lift up. Also, on the plinth, stones have cracked and a portion has fallen down, as if some undue pressure has taken place. I have told the ganger to keep a watch for any developments that may take place; I also think levels should be taken periodically to ascertain what movement is taking place and the cause of the same.
Yours truly, L. Snell

This letter seems to have caused a stir, not surprising considering the urgency of the request, and it was certainly the start of a long period of checks and arguments with the Bargoed Colliery owners.

On 2 January 1922 a number of checks were carried out on the viaduct, the principal reason being that the Bargoed Pit had made workings that were perilously close to the foundations of the viaduct's piers, and in some cases had actually passed beneath the main lines of the Rhymney Railway, as well as the Brecon & Merthyr line. Prior to 1922, the last report regarding coal working in this area had been on 21 April 1917.

The Mining Engineer's reports take up the story:

**7 February 1922:** Northwards, a considerable area worked in Red vein. To fully secure viaduct pillar it should be mentioned that the Brithdir seam had been extensively worked on a pillar and stall system, under the effected portion of the viaduct, and that these later workings in Red vein were calculated to bring about a re-disturbance in those Brithdir old workings. The steady creep and depression that takes place as the result of coal workings sometimes continues for many years after the actual working of the coal; if this injury can be proved to result from workings outside the 40 yards behind, the railway company would be entitled to take action under the Howley Park judgement.

**16 February 1922:** Mr W. G. Griffiths's letter to the General Manager states that up to the present there is little damage. Mr Lawrence, of Lawrence, Davies & Causton, mining engineers, employed on behalf of the railway company, has said that only 40 yards from the railway would cost £10,000 for the purchase of one seam, therefore did not recommend such a course. The maximum distortion or unequal sinking on the east elevation is about 3 inches over the arches, and about 5 inches at the north end (wings) on the west elevation; practically over the arches there is no distortion, but on the north end (wings) there seems to be 'sinking of about 8 inches'. Levels were taken and should be taken every three months.

**23 February 1922:** Inspector Snell reports that movement is accelerating, and there are several cracks under most northern arch.

**24 February 1922:** Mr Holland's inspection, with field glasses, of arch number 1, north end, reveals that joints have opened about 1 inch, and extend from the middle almost to the outside face of the viaduct on the down side; one stone adjoining the keystone has split through the centre. In arch number 4 there are a few open joints around the keystone on the down side, also some small cracks and open joints down the middle of the piers.

Movement had clearly increased and more and more damage was revealed. On 10 June 1922 a report was made out by mining engineers for the Great Western Railway:

'Mining Engineer's report: Some workings in Red vein (added to tracing), advancing rapidly north-eastwards, towards viaduct, depth 612 yards, average thickness 2ft 9in, other seams and depth shown on section, deeper seams not yet proved, probably exist, possibly worked to some extent inside pillar, damage to viaduct slight and comparatively recent, no workings in last three years. Brithdir seam 1907 to 1916 by Rhymney Iron Company: inclined to view that workings in the Brithdir – has seams inside and outside statutory limit – have contributed to damage, average depth of 409 yards, colliery company liability 35 per cent, almost certain further damage from Red vein, some decision needed shortly, depression from Red vein anticipated 1ft 3in or so, while a further subsidence of 2ft 6in will follow the workings of Big vein, now being opened at this colliery.'

On 22 November 1922 these reports, together with others, were discussed by the Great Western Railway at Paddington, and it was decided that the colliery company's percentage for damage would be 35 per cent. Mr Grierson also recommended that purchase of the Bargoed Colliery from the Powell Duffryn Group should not be sought, and steps taken to repair and secure the viaduct, so during 1923 work was started on repairs to Bargoed Viaduct.

In a letter from the Civil Engineer of 9 February 1923, Mr E. H. Hann, General Manager of Powell

*Above*   Bargoed  Viaduct  in  about  1857,  during  its       *Below* Bargoed Viaduct in June 1985, still as picturesque as
construction. *Mrs J. E. Overall*                               when painted by the artist L. S. Lowry in 1965. *Author*

Duffryn, stated that workings in Red vein had stopped, following a meeting with Mr Lawrence on 5 February. On 10 September 1924 costs of £117 for pointing and 10 tons of concrete used on the northern arch were reported, the work being completed on 26 October.

Meanwhile a careful check was kept on the remaining pillars of the viaduct and especially the colliery seams, which were now causing problems not only to the Rhymney Railway, but also to the Brecon & Merthyr, so the mining engineer's reports and checks were taken every two months On 24 June 1924 it was reported that the Red vein was partially worked, and the depression of the Brecon & Merthyr and Rhymney railways was about 12 inches. The Red vein was already partially worked under both lines. The Gilfach Colliery shaft should support the railway, but the pit's pillars were hardly sufficient to support it.

By 1928 there were more reports of subsidence to the railway lines, not only from shaft workings from the Bargoed Pits, but also from the Gilfach, Britannia and Groesfaen collieries, as the mining engineer reported:

**February 1930:** Clay seam discontinued January 1928, and re-opened about May 1929; extraordinarily rapid progress northwards towards the viaduct, the intention being to advance at a higher rate in six months time, when sufficient length of face is opened under the viaduct, at a depth of about 654 yards. These workings will probably effect the viaduct in the same manner as the Red vein.

**12 March 1930:** Colliery company asks for £50,000 compensation for coal lost.

**21 March 1930:** Letter from J. C. Blundell, of the Divisional Engineer's Office, GWR Queen Street, Cardiff, states: Foundations on bed of Pennant Rock, 50 to 55 yards thickness, other bands of strong rock between top Pennant and coal seams, masonry substantial and good, proven of ample thickness, seams of coal already worked under it and, from levels taken, appears to have subsided about 2ft 4in, not in any way affecting the structure to date.

**7 July 1930:** Local change in direction of clay seam, comparatively slow progress southwards, working northwards of this point still in progress, and this may result in seam being worked in a manner to cause unequal depression, and greater damage to the viaduct. It is desirable that this viaduct should be protected without delay.

**31 November 1930:** Clay seam rapidly moving westwards towards viaduct position, some movement may be observed at any time, particularly in northern portion. Advisable to proceed with protection.

**2 December 1930:** Bridge number 69, Bargoed Viaduct, Permanent Way Inspector (PWI) reports that a quarter-inch crack has appeared along work in south end of viaduct, old crack re-opened, some slight movement in the foundation retaining wall, built at end of viaduct pilaster, could see no indication of movement of viaduct itself, cemented up and padded, 1 January 1931.

**5 June 1931:** Two coping stones badly laminated and lifting; fixed 18 June 1931.

**9 February 1932:** Upper four level, towards viaduct and Bargoed station, with normal progress, may be effected in six months time from workings in this seam. Re-levelled the B&M line, clay seam approaching from east, gradual subsidence should result.

**10 May 1933:** PWI reports further cracks in arch at north end.

**7 July 1933:** PWI reports coping on parapet was lifted slightly, pier at north end on up side slightly moved.

**14 July 1933:** Clay seam northwards, slight movement to Darran branch.

**11 August 1933:** Letter from J. C. Blundell: principal movement in first arch at Brithdir end, timber struts to be fixed at springing level, tie bars through spandrel walls, masonry grouted and pointed, loose stones in the two northern arches to be reset.

On 5 February 1934 it was recorded that the fresh workings that had been opened were stopped in September 1933 due to bad roof conditions caused by water from the strata above; the fresh workings north-eastwards within a short distance of the southern end of viaduct would probably cause, in the near future, a gradual movement at the southern end.

By the end of 1934, and with checks varying between five and three times every year until 1945, some slight movement was recorded, but as most reports stated no structural movement to Bargoed Viaduct, it seems that the long battle to rectify the damage caused by the collieries undermining the foundations was finally over.

Today, regular maintenance checks at frequent intervals are carried out, and no evidence of subsidence is noticeable on the viaduct.

Mr John Bateman was born on 7 March 1831, and when he died at 83 years of age in 1914 he was one of the oldest inhabitants of the village of Marazion, Cornwall. In his obituary, *The Cornishman* newspaper reported that 'early in his life he became a railway contractor, in the bridges and stations department, and did a considerable amount of work in the making of the Rhymney Railway, especially in the construction and building of the Bargoed and Crumlin viaducts. After a strenuous life in this country, at 60 years of age, he went to South Africa, and with his son entered into business as a contractor at Pretoria and Johannesburg, under the Boer regime. At that period he became personally acquainted with President Kruger, and other leading Boers. On his retirement from this business, he returned to Marazion in 1899, and settled at Rhymney Villa, which he had provided for himself many years before. He was of a very retiring disposition and the sweets of public life had no attractions for him, although he could have adorned many a position; he was a good old-fashioned Methodist, of a school now fast passing away. Notwithstanding his great age he retained all his faculties up to the last, and a great measure of physical activity and smartness until a few days before his death.' He is pictured in about 1910. *Courtesy of Mrs J. E. Overall*

## Quakers Yard viaducts

Because of the consternation felt concerning the extent of the colliery workings under the viaducts in the South Wales coalfields, especially in the light of the problems encountered with the Bargoed Viaduct, a careful check was kept in the 1920s on the former Taff Vale Extension Viaduct ('No 37'), also referred to as the Vale of Neath Viaduct, which is not quite correct, as well as the former Rhymney Railway and Great Western Railway Joint Viaduct ('No 2'), which carried the line to Merthyr.

The engineer's report on the workings of the Deep Navigation and Treharris Pits regarding the Rhymney Railway and Great Western Railway Joint Viaduct at Quakers Yard in August 1924, stated that 'two districts, one southwards and away from the railway, the other westwards towards the viaducts of the Vale of Neath (Taff Vale Extension) and Rhymney joint lines, support left in 1922, future intentions not yet available, require careful watching'.

On 20 December 1924 the mining engineer's letter to the Secretary stated that if the workings did not advance more rapidly, the intended period before damage occurred to all three viaducts – Vale of Neath, Quakers Yard TVR ('No 68'), and the RR & GWR Joint – was nine months or more. On 20 October 1925 a new seam was reported under the Taff Bargoed branch, but a further report of 27 February 1927 stated that owing to the General Strike the collieries had been idle for seven months, so there was little progress to report. A letter from Mr J. C. Blundell to the Civil Engineer of 13 December 1927 said that timber ribs were placed under the arches, so arranged that installation could take place without undue strain on the strutting.

At a further meeting at Paddington on Tuesday

20 December 1927 it was decided that precautionary measures should be taken, securing the supporting pillars, and also that preventive work should be carried out:

'Pillars of support can be secured clear of present workings on the three viaducts at a cost of £60,000, and preventive work to be undertaken, consists of construction of culverts, doing away with the Merthyr Viaduct altogether, and constructing a new loop from western end of Aberdare Viaduct (Vale of Neath), steel centrings, longitudinal strengthening in arches of various viaducts to secure additional support and elasticity in event of substantial subsidence taking place. Approximate cost of steel centrings from £10,000 to £20,000, maximum liability clause £21,000 for viaducts.'

On the following day another meeting took place at Paddington, and all agreed that it was not practical to construct a solid embankment, or to do away with the RR & GWR Joint viaduct either, and the only practical method would be to use timber strutting and not steel, as was first suggested at a cost of £15,000 for each structure. The work would take six months, so the go-ahead was given for timbers to be placed in position before the commencement of any subsidence.

The work commenced in January 1930, with the first three spans completed by the end of July; thereafter the work was completed at the rate of one span in each viaduct per half year. The cost of the material for the three viaducts came to a total of £1440 14s 2d, which with wages made a grand total of £4046 7s 11d. These costs were originally paid by the Great Western Railway, then the

A postcard view of the Taff Vale c1932. The viaduct just left of centre is the Taff Vale Extension viaduct, and that on the extreme left is the Rhymney Railway and Great Western Railway Joint, both crossing the River Taff at Quakers Yard. It can be seen that both viaducts are shored up with wooden props, which stayed in the arches for many years due to the unsafe foundations under both structures. On the extreme right can be seen the Taff Vale Railway's viaduct. *Author's collection*

colliery companies were charged £4353 12s 9d for the work done.

A Locomotive Inspector's report dated 14 October 1930 described the method of working:

'Working of steam cranes, numbers 2 and 74, operation carried out successfully on 12 October 1930, in steam 5am, operation completed and cranes back in sidings, ready to be packed and prepared for home by 4pm. The girders had to be swung out at 12 ft 0in from the viaduct to clear timber projections that were already in position, then skewed and directed into position at the viaduct pier's base, when they were clear and below these timber obstructions. Girders 66 ft 9 in at 15 tons, 55 feet at 14 tons, 52 feet at 11 tons. The number 2 crane, working with a single rope, still had 12½ turns of rope on the barrel, when the load was down 80 feet, this crane working at 30 feet radius, and number 74 crane working at 26 feet radius would only lower 70 feet, this left only 2½ turns on the barrel, the extra depth being made up with extra slings; this proved a little awkward owing to the limited height of lift between the sleeve head and the girders.'

An early photograph of a 'RR and GWR Joint viaduct' c1905, which spanned the River Taff and enabled this joint line access to the Merthyr Vale Colliery, branching off from what was known as Merthyr Vale Junction, on the Aberfan side of the river. This viaduct was made of steel rather than

A letter to the Civil Engineer of 30 June 1931 gave details of the viaduct and centring:

'Number 2 viaduct (RR and GWR Joint), double line, length 574 feet, straight spars, 5 of 45 feet, 2 of 33 feet, 1 of 50 feet, height of viaduct 100 feet, dated 1884. Timbers used are of pitch pine and laggings are of red deal … Strutting consists of frames eighteen feet in depth, divided into two panels, each panel containing cross bearings, four frames spaced five feet and eight inches, centres are provided in each stage and fixed. The logs forming the horizontal beams and the uprights are fourteen inches – special shipments to Cardiff to deal with the above order.'

However, further problems arose. On 3 September 1931 the river was reported to be undermining the toe of the bank in the south-east corner, and some protection was required for the timber at the bank of the second arch. Floods on 4 November washed out some of the banking from behind the timber and its protection, and it was proposed that a concrete apron be placed above the timbers.

the customary stone, its construction being authorised by an Act of Parliament dated 18 August 1882. It is remembered by railwaymen as they always received the full force of the icy coldness of the wind and rain as they crossed over it. *From The Railway Magazine, 1910*

*Right* A general view of Pontlottyn village looking south, with the station and viaduct in clear view, c1900. *H. F. Jones*

*Below* A '56xx' Class engine crossing the Three Arches Viaduct just after leaving Heath Halt with an up-valley passenger train, c1960. *B. J. Miller collection*

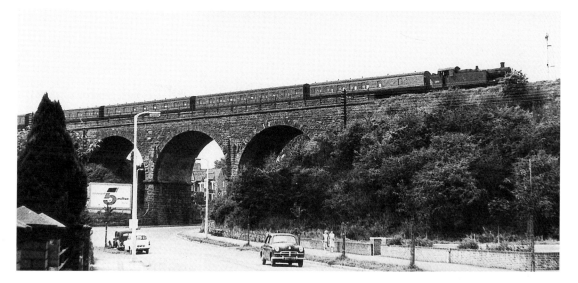

*Below and right* A road bridge over the former Rhymney and Great Western Railway Joint line at the northern end of Aberfan. Clearly seen is the cast iron diamond weight restriction sign, still in place c1961. Such signs were usually found cemented to the walls of road overbridges, or mounted on disused lengths of rail. They only needed an occasional spot of paint on the letters. *I. B. Morris/author's collection*

A 1984 photograph of a pedestrian underpass that allowed the public to cross beneath Energlyn Sidings without risk of trespass or injury. *Author*

In March 1985 DMU set C330 heads up the valley towards Rhymney on the present-day main line, passing under a road bridge near Heath Junction, Cardiff, which is partly steel girders and partly local cut and dressed stone. *Author*

A solitary horse watches as an RCTS railtour, comprising DMU No B576 with B580 at the rear, passes beneath the now preserved bridge at Deri on 14 October 1972. This 'Rhymney No 2' tour from Bristol also visited McClaren Colliery and other locations in the Rhymney Valley. *B. Morris*

# 4. CAERPHILLY LOCOMOTIVE WORKS

In July 1896 the General Manager of the Rhymney Railway Company, Mr Cornelius Lundie, was given permission by the Board of Directors to negotiate with Lord Windsor for the purchase of land on which to build engine, carriage and wagon repair shops. Eventually a site at Wernddu, located midway between Caerphilly Tunnel and the town's station was chosen, and in December 1901 Caerphilly Locomotive Works opened.

On the east side was the engine works, more than 245 feet long and 282 feet wide, which comprised machine, erecting, smiths and boiler shops in numerous bays of varying widths: 42 feet for the machine shop, two bays each of 43 feet for the erecting shops, 35 feet for the testing shop, 42 feet for the smiths shop, 35 feet for the boiler testing shop, and a boiler shop with a bay width of 42 feet.

On the west side was the carriage and wagon shops, which were 220 feet long and 119 feet wide, consisting of wagon, carpenters and paint bays. Partitioned off and sharing two of these bays was the wood machine shop and the wagon sheet shop. The GWR built new carriage shops in 1939.

All of the machinery in these shops, including two 30-ton overhead cranes, was worked by electricity, the current being generated by a duplicate set of compound engines and dynamos.

On 19 September 1962 the British Transport Commission decided to close many railway workshops, and thus save some £3 million. One was Caerphilly, so after a life of 61 years the works closed on 28 June 1963 with the loss of 443 jobs. After many years of disuse it was used as a storage area by the council, then by a variety of firms; today the premises on the east side are occupied by J. J. Castings Ltd.

A single line ran from the goods yard at Caerphilly station to a works platform, used by the workmen's train. In later years, after the closure of the works, the Caerphilly Railway Society took over one of the works yard sidings, of three-eighths of a mile, and ran short steam and diesel trips back and forth along it. The society, formed in 1973, had hopes to purchase the remaining length of track and restore the connection between the works and the station. By 1993 the society's collection comprised six steam and three diesel engines, together with a mixture of wagons and vans, but sadly the society is no more, the stock having been split up and sold off.

Mr Lundie had been born in Kelso, Scotland, in 1815. Prior to this he had been Traffic Manager for the Blyth & Tyne Railway, joining the Rhymney in 1863, and for more than 40 years involved himself in every aspect of railway life, finally achieving the post of General Manager. In 1904, at the age of 89, he retired from that position, only to be elected by the Rhymney Railway as a Director, which meant that nothing changed, and he still acted as before. He died at the grand old age of 93 on 12 February 1908, still in harness.

At the half-yearly meeting of shareholders and directors held at the Angel Hotel, Cardiff, on 7 August 1908, Mr Jennings of the board of shareholders declared that the pay that Mr Lundie would have earned had he lived to the end of that current year be given to his widow, Mrs Ethel Lundie, in grateful recognition of Mr Lundie's services.

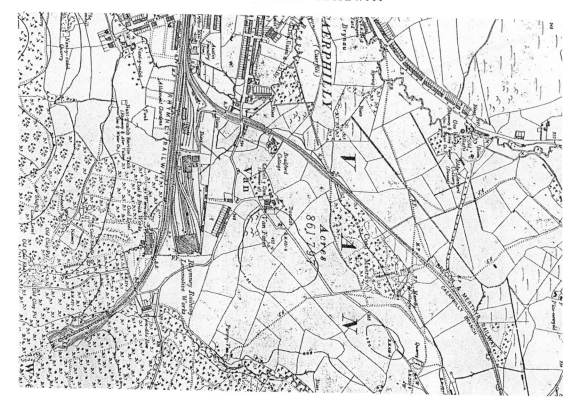

**Above** Caerphilly Works seen from an Ordnance Survey map of 1922. *Crown copyright*

**Left** A corresponding 1950s aerial view of the works. *Caerphilly County Borough Council*

**Top right** The southern part of the works shown on an Ordnance Survey map of 1939. *Crown copyright*

The engine works (*middle right*) and the carriage and wagon shops at Caerphilly, c1905. *From* The Railway Magazine, *1910*

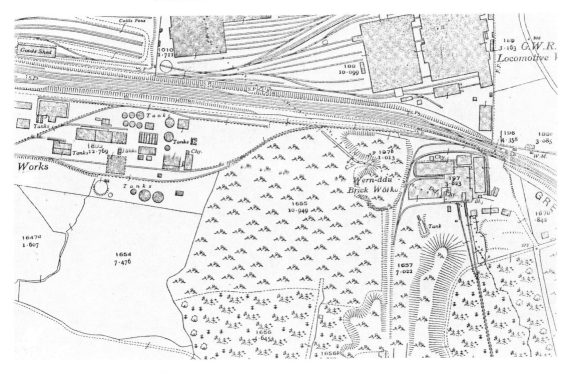

*Above*  This former 'P' Class engine was built in 1921 by Hudswell Clarke, works number 1443, and numbered by the Rhymney Railway as 35. Re-numbered 78 by the GWR, it seen here at Caerphilly Works undergoing an overhaul on 30 August 1934. It was withdrawn from service in 1955. *The Transport Secretary*

*Below*  On the same day a former Taff Vale Railway engine, GWR number 794, is seen inside the works also being overhauled. This 'H' Class engine was built in 1884 by Kitson & Co, works number 2699, and numbered 143 by the TVR. *The Transport Secretary*

*Above* Out in the yard is former Rhymney Railway engine No 36, re-numbered 79 by the GWR. Built by Hudswell Clarke in 1921, works number 1444, this 'P' Class engine has had its steam dome removed, showing the asbestos lining. It was withdrawn in 1955. *The Transport Secretary*

*Below* A Brecon & Merthyr Railway engine, GWR No 888, also photographed on 30 August 1934, stands in Caerphilly Works yard, also with its steam dome removed. Built in 1914 by Robert Stephenson, works number 3578, and numbered 41 by the B&M, it was rebuilt with a GWR tapered boiler in 1941, and withdrawn in 1950. *The Transport Secretary*

# 5. RHYMNEY RAILWAY LOCOMOTIVES

On 31 December 1901 the Rhymney Railway had a total of 105 engines, 100 passenger coaches (which totalled 114 by 1908) and 859 wagons of various types. All the company's original engines were still in service except for Nos 7, 8 and 9, which had been replaced. The mainstay for the passenger services were Nos 62, 63, 64, 65 and 66, but a few saddle tanks were used as needed. Since 1880 the Westinghouse air brake system had been used, but since other local companies used vacuum brakes, a few Rhymney Railway engines were converted to deal with excursion trains. Some of these ran as far afield as Manchester, and were taken over by LNWR engines at Nant-y-bwch, the LNWR only having running rights over the Rhymney for goods trains. The Eames non-

automatic goods brake system was fitted to several Rhymney mineral engines – this American system was not widely used in the British Isles.

No 16, one of the original passenger engines, was due to be withdrawn from stock in 1894, but on Mr Lundie's personal intervention it was reprieved, as it was his favourite engine, and was subsequently used for light passenger work. Kept at the Cardiff Docks engine shed, it was always used in hauling saloon carriage No 5 when the Directors toured the system. When Caerphilly Works opened, No 16 became the first works pilot engine. It finally retired in 1904, but Mr Lundie could not bear it to be broken up, so it was stored in the works test shop. Upon Mr Lundie's death in 1908, no time was wasted in breaking up No 16.

Rhymney Railway 'R' Class engine No 1 is seen here on passenger service at Bargoed station c1910. Built by Robert Stephenson in 1907, works number 3288, it was re-numbered 30 by the GWR and withdrawn in 1949. *Lens of Sutton collection*

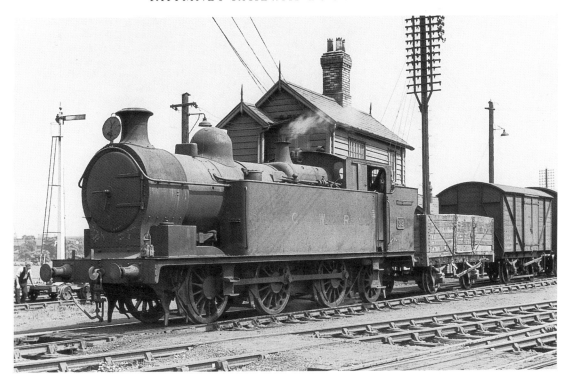

*Above*  No 3 of the Rhymney Railway, seen here with its GWR number 32, was another 'R' Class engine built by Stephenson in 1907, under works number 3290. It is seen here in about 1945 next to Radyr Yard signal box, which was later used as the supervisor's office. *G. W. Sharpe collection*

*Right*  This 'P' Class engine, GWR No 83, was another Stephenson product, works number 3374 of 1909. Originally RR No 6, it is seen here in British Railways livery at Rhymney station in about 1950; it was withdrawn five years later. *G. W. Sharpe collection*

*Right*  In ex-works condition, former Rhymney Railway 'A' Class engine No 14 was later re-numbered 56. A 1910 Stephenson locomotive, works number 3391, it was re-built with a GWR tapered boiler in 1936. Seen here newly painted in British Railways livery at the former TVR Cathays Works in Cardiff on 20 June 1949, it was withdrawn in 1953. *G. W. Sharpe collection*

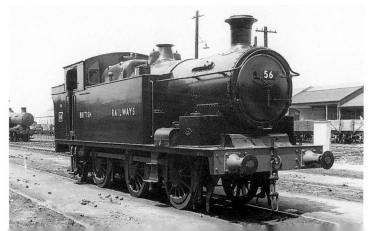

*Top* Rhymney Railway 'M' Class No 16, photographed at Cardiff Docks on 14 August 1924. Built by Robert Stephenson, works number 3130, in 1904, it was re-numbered by the GWR as No 33, and withdrawn some time between 1949 and 1951. *G. W. Sharpe collection*

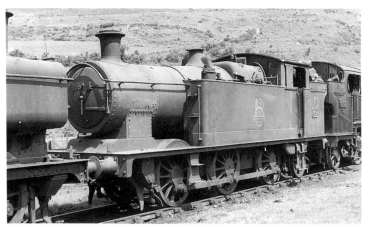

*Middle* Built by Stephenson in 1918, works number 3661, this Rhymney 'A1' Class engine, No 29, is seen here with its GWR number 69 on 7 June 1953 at the Duffryn Yard engine shed of the Port Talbot Railway Company. It was later fitted with a GWR No 10 standard boiler, and was withdrawn in the July of 1955. *F. T. Hornby*

*Bottom* Rhymney Railway 'A' Class No 30 was also built in 1918 by Stephenson, works number 3662. Later GWR No 70, it is seen with a Cardiff to Caerphilly freight train at Heath, Cardiff, on 16 May 1919. *LCGB, Ken Nunn Collection*

*Right* Rhymney Railway saddle tank No 31, seen here in full lining c1890, was built by Sharp Stewart & Co in 1872, works number 2267. This 'G' Class engine shows a good example of the straight type of numberplate. It was withdrawn some time between 1914 and 1921. *Real Photograph Company*

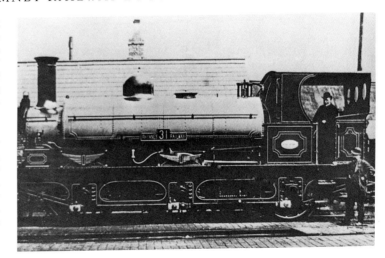

*Below* On 17 May 1919 Rhymney Railway No 31 heads the 3.55pm Cardiff to Rhymney Bridge passenger train near the Heath area of Cardiff. This 'P' Class engine was built by Hudswell Clarke in 1917, works number 1121, and became GWR No 77. It was withdrawn in 1953. *LCGB, Ken Nunn Collection*

*Right* No 38, another 'P' Class 0-6-2T, minus its centre driving wheels, stands at Cardiff East Dock engine shed, in BR livery and with its GWR number 81. Also built by Hudswell Clarke, works number 1457 of 1921, it was photographed on 20 June 1949. *G. W. Sharpe collection*

*Top* Rhymney Railway 'R' Class No 39, GWR No 35, is seen on 7 January 1954 pulling a Llanbradach Colliery train of empty coke wagons along the embankment of Heath High Level. Another Hudswell Clarke engine of 1921, works number 1431, it was withdrawn by British Railways in November 1956.

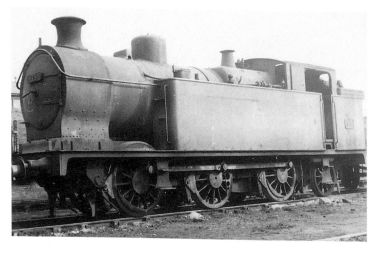

E. L. Ahrons, writing in *The Railway Magazine* of 1923, described how mineral trains descending the valley inclines had to be carefully regulated. Wagon brakes had to be pinned down in sufficient numbers to keep the train under control, but it was strictly upheld that skidding the wheels was to be avoided, and that if any wheel was found to be skidding the guard and brakesman would be severely punished. To prevent the wooden brake blocks from burning when descending a bank, the drivers had to keep their rail water taps open, and guards had instructions to put out any such fires when at the bottom of the incline. Whether it was humanly possible to always avoid the skidding of every wheel is somewhat open to doubt, especially as nearly all the wagon belonged not to the railway company but to the collieries, and their condition was not perfect by any standards. *B. J. Miller collection*

*Middle* 'R' Class No 43, GWR No 39, seen here at Cardiff East Dock on 29 October 1955, was built by Beyer Peacock in 1921, works number 6099. *D. K. Jones collection*

*Bottom* The same engine in rather different surroundings, seen here sadly awaiting scrapping at Swindon Works after being withdrawn from service in November 1956. *F. T. Hornby*

*Above* 'R' Class No 41, later GWR No 37, heads a Cardiff Docks to Bargoed Pits train through Cefn On Halt on 12 August 1952. Built by Hudswell Clarke in 1921, works number 1438, it was withdrawn in 1956. *B. J. Miller collection*

*Below* Another 'R' Class 0-6-2T, photographed on 26 January 1957, this time with a Nantgarw Colliery to Cardiff Docks mineral train. This locomotive was also built by Hudswell Clarke in 1921, works number 1439; originally No 42, it later became GWR No 38. *B. J. Miller collection*

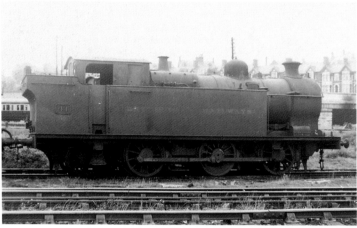

*Above* On 30 May 1955 the former 'R' Class No 46, re-numbered as 42 by the GWR, hauls a train of up empties past Heath Junction; on the right are the former Rhymney Railway carriage sidings. Built by Beyer Peacock in 1921, works number 6102, this engine was withdrawn in 1957. *B. J. Miller collection*

*Left* A profile view of 'R' Class No 45 (GWR No 41) at Barry engine sheds on 11 June 1949. Built by Beyer Peacock in 1921, works number 6101, it lasted until 1956. *The late N. L. Browne, courtesy of F. T. Hornby*

*Left* A picturesque view of 'R' Class No 47 (later GWR No 43) at Cefn On Halt on 31 March 1956 with a Cwm Bargoed to Cardiff freight. Another Beyer Peacock product of 1921, works number 6103, it was withdrawn in 1957. *B. J. Miller collection*

*Top* Carrying its GWR number 44, 'R' Class engine No 62 (Beyer Peacock works number 6104 of 1921) is at Swindon Works in 1956 awaiting scrapping after being withdrawn in July of that year. *F. T. Hornby*

*Middle* A c1912 portrait of Rhymney Railway No 64, built at the Vulcan Foundry in 1890, works number 1291. This 'L' Class engine, originally of a 2-4-2 design, was rebuilt as a 0-6-2 saddle tank in 1906. The number is in the final Rhymney style, with painted letters and numbers. Clearly seen is the Westinghouse pump on the side of the smokebox. The engine was later re-numbered by the GWR as 150. *B. Morris*

*Bottom* Two for one: Rhymney Railway 'J' Class No 70 pilots No 118 on a Cardiff to Caerphilly freight train at Heath South Junction on 11 August 1913. No 70 was built at the Vulcan Foundry in 1891, works number 1332, becoming GWR No 100 and being withdrawn from service between 1925 and 1934. 'A' Class No 118 (GWR No 74) was built by Robert Stephenson in 1910, works number 3395. *LCGB, Ken Nunn Collection*

*Above* 'K' Class No 74 (built by Sharp Stewart in 1895, works number 4042, and later GWR No 107) is seen with the 8.00pm Cardiff to Merthyr train passing Heath Junction on 16 May 1919. *LCGB, Ken Nunn Collection*

*Left* Another 'K' Class 0-6-2ST, No 83 (later GWR No 118) was built in 1897 by Sharp Stewart, works number 513, and was withdrawn between 1925 and 1934. *RAS Marketing*

*Left* Rhymney Railway 'S' Class No 113 (later GWR No 95) was built by Hudswell Clarke in 1908, works number 848. Its speed slightly defeating the lens at Heath Sidings, Cardiff, on 17 May 1919, it is running light, possibly on banking duties. *LCGB, Ken Nunn Collection*

# 6. ROLLING-STOCK

Six-wheeled passenger vehicles were in the majority, although in 1900 the Rhymney bought from the Gloucester Carriage & Wagon Company stock consisting of Bogie Composites Nos 87, 88, 89 and 90, and eight Bogie 3rds, Nos 91-98; the rest of the stock consisted of ten Composites, 54 3rds, one Brake 3rd, 19 mineral brake-vans, one horse box, two carriage trucks and a saloon carriage; the carriage trucks and horse box had through Westinghouse and vacuum pipes for working over other companies' lines. By January 1910 the company's coaching stock consisted of one Saloon, two steam railmotor cars, 21 1st/2nd Composites, and 67 3rd Class carriages. These were all fitted with electric light and Westinghouse brakes.

The old four-wheelers used on workmen's trains were never included in the passenger stock lists.

The GWR broke up most of the older stock shortly after the Grouping, and those that survived were altered to vacuum braking. Generally the bogie carriages lasted well into British Railways days, albeit used as workmen's carriages, placed at the rear of valley trains, and pressed into service for football specials to Ninian Park and excursions to Barry Island; such carriages saw service until late 1958.

The total number of passengers carried over the years increased greatly: in 1897 a total of 1,500,000 were carried, but by 1902 this number had increased to 3,500,000, the receipts amounting to £34,000 in 1897, and reaching £76,000 by 1908, a tremendous amount for a company that only had 62 miles of running lines, not all of which carried passenger services, only mineral traffic.

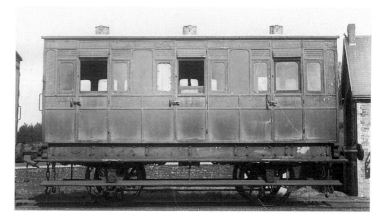

**Rhymney Railway coach No 1 at Caerphilly Works on 23 March 1913.** *LCGB, Ken Nunn Collection*

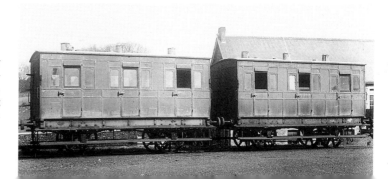

**Coaches Nos 1 and 2 at Caerphilly Works on the same day. Both of a four-wheeled, three-compartment design, these coaches were used at the opening of the railway in 1858.** *LCGB, Ken Nunn Collection*

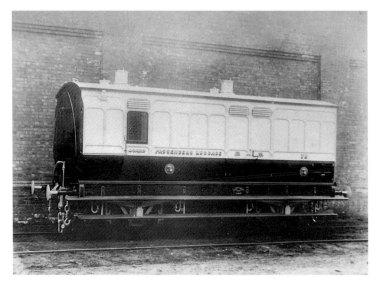

*Left* A Rhymney Railway Passenger Luggage van, c1880. Clearly seen are the safety chains, fitted on either side of the main couplings; eventually these were found to be unnecessary and were removed around the turn of the 20th century. *M. Lloyd*

*Below* Built as Rhymney Railway 24-ton coach No 56 in 1920 by the Gloucester Carriage & Wagon Company, this vehicle was later numbered W1090, and was photographed in Rhymney station sidings on 6 June 1953. *F. T. Hornby*

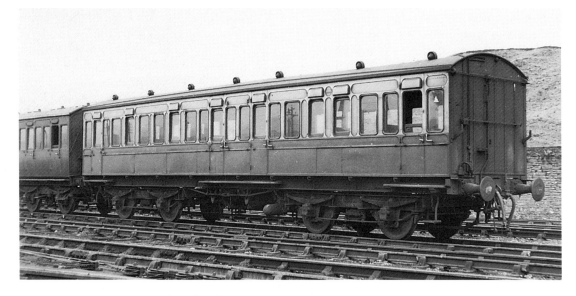

*Left* Rhymney Railway two-plank iron-ore wagons at the East Bute Docks, Cardiff, around the turn of the 20th century. The wagon under the crane is fitted with an early type of 'dumb buffers'. *M. Lloyd*

# 7. MISCELLANEA

**RHYMNEY RAILWAY.—NOTICE.**

TICKETS at REDUCED FARES for the DOUBLE JOURNEY will be issued at all the Stations on this Railway to CARDIFF, on MONDAY, MAY 31st, and TUESDAY, JUNE 1st, the days on which the EISTEDDFOD and CONCERT will be held in Cardiff; and on WEDNESDAY, THURSDAY, and FRIDAY, June 2nd, 3rd, and 4th, the Days of the BATH & WEST OF ENGLAND SOCIETY'S MEETING, at Cardiff.

To and Fro Tickets will only be available for the day of issue; but Return Tickets will be issued on May 31st, June 2nd and 3rd, available for the Return Journey the following Day.

Further information can be obtained by applying at any of the Stations.

By Order,
W. R. PAGE, Traffic Manager.
Cardiff, May 26th, 1858.

---

**BATH AND WEST OF ENGLAND SOCIETY'S MEETING IN CARDIFF.**

**JUNE 2ND, 3RD, AND 4TH, 1858.**

Direct Route to Cardiff from the Midland Counties and the North, without break of gauge, *via* Shrewsbury, Hereford Pontypool Road, and Rhymney Railway.

**RHYMNEY RAILWAY.**
**NOTICE.**

ON JUNE 2nd, 3rd, and 4th, 1858, TICKETS, at CHEAP FARES, for the Double Journey, will be issued at all the Stations to CARDIFF, available only for the day of issue.

Return Tickets, at Reduced Fares, will also be issued at all the Stations, on June 2nd and 3rd, available for the Return Journey upon the following days.

LIVE STOCK, IMPLEMENTS, and POULTRY, will be charged Half the usual Rates from the different Stations on the Line to Cardiff, and the same on return, if unsold; and if sold, the usual rates.

The Live Stock, Implements, and Poultry, must be loaded at all the Stations not later than one clear day, before the day of admission to the Yard. Persons in charge of these, may travel at a Single Third Class Fare from any Station to Cardiff, such Fares to be available for the Return Journey for Three days after the Show.

By Order,
W. R. PAGE,
Traffic Manager.
Cardiff, May 19th, 1858.

---

STEAM COMMUNICATION BETWEEN

**RHYMNEY RAILWAY.**
**ALTERATION OF PASSENGER TRAINS.**

ON and after Monday, July 5th, 1858, the 9h. 45m. Morning Train from ADAM STREET STATION. CARDIFF, will leave at 9h. 20m., arriving in Rhymney at 10h. 50m., and the 9h. 45m. Morning Train from Rhymney will leave at 9h. 40m., arriving at Cardiff at 11h. 10m.

TOURIST TICKETS are issued at Cardiff to Killarney *via* Shrewsbury, Stafford, Chester, and Holyhead; by the Express or Mail boats to Kingstown; by the Dublin and Kingstown Railway, to Dublin; by the Great Southern and Western Railway, from Dublin to Cork; and back to Mallow for Killarney, by the Killarney Junction Railway; returning from Mallow by the same route, at any time not exceeding one month from the date of issue. The Tourist can break the journey at Chester, Bangor, Holyhead, Dublin, Cork, and Mallow.

FARES, First Class, £5 15s. Second Class, £4 15s.

The Holder is also entitled to have issued to him, Tickets at Reduced Fares, available for seven days. 1.—At the offices of the Dublin and Drogheda Company, Amien-street Dublin, Dublin to Belfast and back, for the tour to the Giant's Causeway. 2.—At the offices of the Midland Great Western Company, Broadstairs, Dublin, Dublin to Galway and back, for the tour to Connemara. 3.—At each Terminus of the Cork and Bandon Railway; at the Kenmare Arms Hotel, Killarney; and Roche's Hotel, Glengariffe; for the tour between Cork and Killarney, *via* the Cork and Bandon Railway, Bantry, Glengariffe, and Kenmare, each day (Sundays excepted). Second Class Rail, 18s. First Class Rail, 1s. extra.

NOTE.—The Tickets are forfeited if transferred.

By Order,
W. R. PAGE, Traffic Manager.
Cardiff, 28th June, 1858.

Early newspaper announcements from the *Cardiff & Merthyr Guardian* of May (*left*) and July 1858. *South Glamorgan Libraries*

Rhymney Railway letter stamp of the type issued for use in February 1891, reproduced at actual size. *J. C. Haydon*

# Signals

# Notices

*Right* A bilingual Welsh and English Rhymney Railway trespass sign at Bargoed station, photographed on 13 November 1962. *G. Pearce*

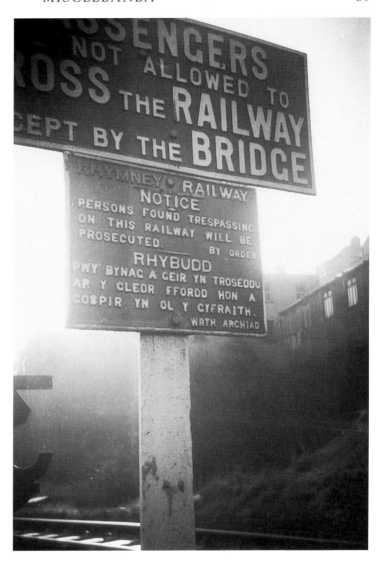

*Below* A Rhymney Railway trespass notice. *C. Hughes collection*

*Below* A weight restriction sign (see also page 70). *GWR Staff Association Club, Merthyr Tydfil*

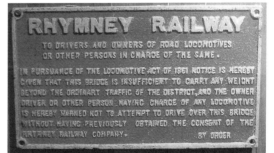

# Accidents

A collision on the Rhymney Railway at Brithdir, June 1904. *Starling Press*

During January 1925 the Rhymney Valley, together with other areas of South Wales, was devastated by heavy rain that swamped fields and roads alike, and on 3 January the inevitable happened. On 10 January 1925 the *Cardiff Times* reported 'RAILWAY SMASH AT TIRPHIL – A disastrous railway accident occurred between Tirphil and Brithdir on Saturday last, as a result of the heavy rains.' It went on:

### 'Driver And Fireman Killed

### Rhymney Train Over Embankment

A mineral train travelling in the direction of Bargoed toppled over the embankment between Tirphil and Brithdir stations on the Rhymney branch of the GWR early on Saturday morning. The engine driver and his fireman were killed, but the guard escaped without injury. The two victims are George Cooper, St Helens Road, Abergavenny, driver, William Morris, North Road, Abergavenny, fireman. The guard who escaped is William Haines, of North Road, Abergavenny.

The train, which belonged to the London and North Western Railway Company, comprised of an engine and 16 vans. It was travelling down the line in the direction of Bargoed, and when about half a mile from Tirphil station the line apparently gave way, and the engine tumbled over the embankment, taking with it many of the trucks. The engine is now embedded in the clay soil near the river below, and the unfortunate driver and fireman are pinned beneath it. The guards van and several wagons are topsy-turvy on the engine below. It appears that an old coal level was worked in the vicinity of the accident some years ago.

The disaster stopped traffic on the line, which is badly damaged. This disaster is presumed to have been caused by the earth being washed away by the heavy rain. Breakdown gangs and ambulance workers immediately proceeded to the scene. A graphic description of the accident was given to the *South Wales News* representative by Councillor John Wilkins, of New Tredegar, who apparently is the only man alive, beside the guard, who saw

The accident at Tirphil on 3 January 1925. The engine was LNWR No 607. The *Cardiff Times* reported '...some of the wagons, several of which tumbled down the embankment, can be observed perched in a perilous position on top of the embankment.' Cardiff Times

The wreckage at the foot of the railway embankment. Cardiff Times

the occurrence. "I was going to my work," said Mr Wilkins, "when I heard a train coming down the line. All of a sudden I heard a terrific crash, accompanied by flashes of fire and flame, and looking round the other side of the river, I saw a train toppling over the embankment. I hurried to the scene but for a long time I could not see a soul. Eventually I saw the guard who had escaped because his van had kept to the rails. I made a more minute inspection and found near the river the engine deeply embedded in the clay soil, and underneath the engine were the engine driver and fireman, both dead at the time, in my opinion.'

## Coaches Telescoped

The South Wales Weekly News representative visited the scene, and found some of the coaches telescoped and others smashed to bits. A 50-ton crane and a plant of acetylene welders had arrived and some of the damaged coaches had already been removed. Some of the coaches are a mass of ruin on the engine. The two victims were pinned down underneath the engine by their legs, and it is believed they were probably trying to make their escape when they were caught. It is presumed that the engine driver was killed instantaneously, as he sustained a serious wound. The engine driver's watch had stopped, but the fireman's watch was going after the accident.

### Collieries Stopped

In consequence of the disaster, between 2000 and 3000 men employed at Mardy Pit, Rhymney, and the New Tredegar Colliery, in Tredegar, were rendered idle. When the train fell over the embankment it appears that an electric standard was struck and the wires severed, cutting off the supply of electricity from the Bargoed Power Station to these two collieries. In the case of the New Tredegar Colliery the ventilation fans were stopped.

### Victims' Bodies Removed

### Surgeon's Grim Task

After two days hard work, the bodies of the engine driver and fireman victims of the Brithdir train disaster on Saturday morning were recovered from under the wrecked engine on Monday morning. Owing to the fact that the unfortunate men were pinned by the legs, those limbs had to be amputated before the bodies could be extricated. The amputation operation was performed by Dr F. I. Maunsell and E. T. Irving. They were hampered in the operations because the men were huddled up, and the surgeons had to crawl into the cab of the engine. In the opinion of Dr Maunsell the

In about 1960 former GWR '56xx' Class 0-6-2T No 6638 ran away with a train of coal wagons while descending the 'Big Hill', as the Walnut Tree branch was affectionately known by railwaymen, and was derailed at the sand trap at Taffs Well. The photographs demonstrate very well the life-saving facility of these sand traps in harmlessly stopping a runaway without serious damage to loco or stock. No 6638 was built in 1937, and withdrawn in 1962. *J. Morgan collection*

men were suffocated by steam and died within a few minutes of the accident.'

Also on that fateful Saturday, 3 January 1925, there was another serious derailment, again caused by the heavy rain. The *Cardiff Times* reported:

'On Saturday afternoon a slight landslide occurred on the Rhymney Railway between Ystrad Mynach and Penalltau Colliery, at Penrhiwfelin. The line is only used for mineral traffic, so that there was no disorganisation of traffic.'

It was quite a month, and it was not only the Rhymney Railway that was affected. At Pontsticill, on the Brecon & Merthyr Railway, a train was caught in a landslide and passengers had to leave their carriages and walk along the outside of the train to safety.

More recent mishaps on Rhymney lines: this Class 37 came to grief on points at Ystrad Mynach South Junction in about 1970. *B. Morris*

Another Class 37 off the tracks at Ystrad Mynach South Junction, in about 1972. *B. Morris*

# ACKNOWLEDGEMENTS

I must thank Alun Powell for finding the time to write the Foreword, and his good wife Val for being such an excellent hostess.

I would also like to thank the many people whom I have met, and express appreciation for the warm letters and treasured photographs that have been sent; I am grateful for the chance to copy and return them. Thanks also to those photographers who set out in all kinds of weather to capture a scene that nobody but a few realised would change as much as it has. I have tried to record the scene of today, and mix it with memories of the past, but without the help of others, and the guidance of our libraries and museums, the task would have been impossible.

Thanks, therefore, to the following individuals: Mr L. D. Bryant, Bridgend; Mr A. Burton (Pontypridd Public Library); Mr H. Bux (Oddfellows Club, Cardiff); Mr R. S. Carpenter, Birmingham (Lens of Sutton collection); Mr A. Carreg, Aberamen; Mr R. M. Casserley, Berkhamsted; Mr C. Chapman, Hinckley; Mr T. D. Chapman, Aberamen; Mr V. Crabb, Pontypridd; Mr J. J. Davis, Torquay; Mr M. Davies, Merthyr Tydfil; Mr J. Dore Dennis, Westra; Mr R. L. Edwards (Cardiff Public Library); Mr M. Farquhar, Portland; Mr D. A. Francis (Merthyr Tydfil Public Library); Mr M. Hale, Dudley; Mr C. W. Harris, Porth; Mrs Y. M. Harris (Caerphilly County Borough Council); Mrs E. Hart (Illustrated London News Library, London); Mr J. C. Haydon, Reading; Mr B. Hoper, Insch (The Transport Secretary); Mr F. T. Hornby, North Cheam; Mr C. Hughes, Abercynon; Mr G. James (Merthyr Tydfil Public Library); Mr D. K. Jones, Mountain Ash; Mr H. F. Jones, Pontlottyn; Mr P. Korrison, St Albans; Mr H. Leadbetter, Upton Wirral; Mr M. E. Ling (Cardiff Public Library); Mrs H. Lloyd Fernandez (ABP, Cardiff); Mr M. Lloyd, Hereford; Mr B. J. Miller, Barry; Mr J. Morgan, Cardiff; Mr B. Morris, Merthyr Tydfil;

Mrs J. E. Overall, Caterham; Mr M. O'Connel, GWR Staff Assoc Club, Cardiff; Mr G. Pearce, Cardiff; Mr S. C. L. Phillips, c/o Mr D. K. Jones, Mountain Ash; Mr A. Powell, Rhydyfelin; Mr K. Ryan, Pontypridd; Mrs S. Scott (Rhondda Borough Libraries); Mr G. W. Sharpe, Barnsley; Mrs J. Smith, (Associated British Ports, Cardiff); Mr G. Stacey, Egham (RAS Marketing, LCGB Collection); Mr E. J. Starr, Caerphilly; Mr C. Thomas (Deputy Port Manager, ABP, Cardiff); Mr D. G. Thomas, London; Mr T. Underwood (Oddfellows Club, Cardiff); Mr D. Watkins, Merthyr Tydfil; and Mrs E. Williams, Caerphilly.

Thanks also to: Caerphilly Public Library; Cardiff Public Library; Cynon Valley Libraries; Great Western Railway Staff Association Club, Cardiff; Great Western Railway Staff Association Club, Merthyr Tydfil; Merthyr Tydfil Public Libraries; Mid Glamorgan Libraries; Locomotive Club of Great Britain; Locomotive and General Railway Photographs Company; Oddfellows Club, Cardiff; Ordnance Survey Department, Southampton; Real Photographs Company, Weybridge; Rhondda Borough Libraries; South Glamorgan Libraries, for permission to use extracts from the *Cardiff & Merthyr Guardian*.

Thanks to Mr G. Body of Avon Anglia Publications, for permission to use the late C. R. Clinker's register of closed stations and halts, also with the permission of the widow of the late C. R. Clinker.

To Mr G. G. Jones, for his permission to use extracts from his thesis on the history of Caerphilly, with reference to the collieries in the Rhymney Valley, extracts from the Journal of the Caerphilly Local History Society, and extracts he kindly sent me from his *Cronicl Caerffili* Nos 5 and 6, and from the *Cardiff Times*.

To Mr Kichenside, editor, David & Charles publishers, for permission to use opening and closing dates of stations.

To the editor of the Illustrated London News Library, London, for permission to use the sketch of the Bute East Dock Extension.

To the editor of the Oakwood Press, for permission to use opening dates of stations, halts and junctions from the excellent work by Mr D. S. M. Barrie.

To Mr J. Slater, of *The Railway Magazine*, for his permission to use extracts and captions from the 1910, 1912, 1923 and 1924 editions of the magazine.

To Mr R. A. Storey and M. A. G. Tough of the University of Warwick Library and Modern Records Centre, and to the Secretary of the National Union of Railwaymen, London, for their permission to use the TVR strike telegram of 1900.

To Joyce, widow of the late Norman Browne, of Surrey, a gentleman and a good railway photographer.

To the memory of Mr Glyn Davies of Aberdare, a good local, historical and industrial photographer.

To the widow of the late John A. Owen, for the use of his photographic collection on Dowlais Works.

To the widow of the late Norman Parry, a member of the GWR Staff Association Club, Merthyr Tydfil.

To the memory of Mr John Phelps, former employee of ABP, Cardiff, a good man and friend to all.

To the widow of the late Sid Rickard, another gentleman, whose passing marks the end of an era.

To the memory of Mr John Smith, of Lens of Sutton, another sad loss, but whose collection lives on.

# INDEX